"A Paradise for Boys and Girls"

"A Paradise for Boys and Girls"

CHILDREN'S CAMPS IN THE
ADIRONDACKS

Hallie E. Bond

Joan Jacobs Brumberg

and Leslie Paris

With a Foreword by Philip G. Terrie

THE ADIRONDACK MUSEUM/SYRACUSE UNIVERSITY PRESS

Library of Congress Cataloging-in-Publication Data

Bond, Hallie E.

"A paradise for boys and girls" : children's camps in the Adirondacks / Hallie E. Bond, Joan Jacobs Brumberg, and Leslie Paris ; with a foreword by Philip G. Terrie.— 1st ed.

p. cm.

Includes bibliographical references and index.

ISBN 0–8156–0822–5 (alk. paper)

1. Camps—New York (State)—Adirondack Mountains—History. 2. Children—New York (State)—Adirondack Mountains—History. I. Brumberg, Joan Jacobs. II. Paris, Leslie. III. Title.

GV194.N7B66 2006

796.54'20974753—dc22

2006001683

Manufactured in the United States of America

HALLIE E. BOND has been curator at the Adirondack Museum since 1987. She curated the temporary exhibit A Paradise for Boys and Girls, which opened in 2003, and the permanent exhibit Boats and Boating in the Adirondacks (1991); the companion volume *Boats and Boating in the Adirondacks* was published by Syracuse University Press in 1995. Bond holds an M.A. in medieval studies from the University of York (United Kingdom), as well as an M.A. in American history and a certificate in museum studies from the University of Delaware, where she was a Hagley Fellow.

JOAN JACOBS BRUMBERG is Stephen H. Weiss Presidential Fellow and professor of history, human development, and gender studies at Cornell University. Her books *Kansas Charlie: The Story of a Nineteenth-Century Boy Murderer* (2004), *The Body Project: An Intimate History of American Girls* (1997), and *Fasting Girls: A History of Anorexia Nervosa as a Modern Disease* (1988) have explored different aspects of the history of childhood. She holds a Ph.D. in history from the University of Virginia and an M.A. in American studies from Boston College. She grew up spending summers at Adirondack camps where her father was employed.

LESLIE PARIS is assistant professor at the University of British Columbia. She was project historian for the Adirondack Museum's 2003 exhibit A Paradise for Boys and Girls. Paris has published numerous articles on the history of girlhood and summer camps, and her doctoral dissertation, "Children's Nature: Summer Camps in New York State, 1919–1941," will be published in 2006. She earned a Ph.D. from the University of Michigan in 2000.

Contents

Foreword

DESPITE THE BANALITY of institutional food, the tortures of blackflies and mosquitoes, and the slippery black mud of Adirondack trails, thousands upon thousands of girls and boys and young women and men who attended or worked at Adirondack camps came back for more. As campers and counselors, they spent nights in damp sleeping bags and endured the cruelties that children and teenagers inevitably visit upon one another. Yet, as adults, many say that the camp experience was one of the most positive of their lives. Learning to swim in water uncorrupted by the stench of chlorine, spending a month or so away from television and even electricity (not to mention parents and siblings), bagging the forty-six peaks—these and countless other adventures were formative.

I first crossed the Blue Line in June 1966, on a chartered bus to Long Lake, where I was to be a counselor at Adirondack Wilderness Camp (AWC). I was seventeen, just a few weeks out of high school, and had very little idea of where I was going or what I would do there. As a child, I had been a camper myself—for five summers, on the banks of the Cowpasture River in the mountains of western Virginia—and thus had some notion of what the camp experience was all about. But I hadn't the faintest inkling of what the Adirondacks would come to mean to me. Stumbling upon that summer job, which I had secured just a month or so earlier, turned out to be one of the pivotal points in my life.

Before the summer was over, I'd bushwhacked from Couchsachraga to Panther (long before there was a herd path) and had fallen utterly in love with the Adirondacks. I eagerly committed to returning the next year and came back each summer until economic realities forced the camp's closing after the 1971 season. Now pushing sixty, I'm still spending July and August—and as many weekends as I can hustle—on Long Lake, only a couple of miles from the spot where AWC filled the summers of my college years with friendship and planted the seeds of both environmentalism and a passion for all things Adirondack.

At AWC, the guiding philosophy reflected a conviction that the Adirondack wilderness itself was every camper's best teacher. Camp director Elliott Verner, along with his brother, Bill Verner (a curator at the Adirondack Museum, which let him take the summers off), aimed to have every boy spend as much time as possible in the woods. This meant that the older boys, of about twelve to fourteen, were finishing the summer with backpacking trips that lasted two weeks. Many years later, it still amazes me that I was actually paid good money to lead these expeditions, to spend day after day climbing in the High Peaks, swimming in cold brooks on hot days, and slowly meandering from Keene Valley back to Long Lake. It was a summer job that most people could only dream of.

In this volume, Leslie Paris, Hallie Bond, and Joan Jacobs Brumberg have combined cultural and social history to tell us how Adirondack camps began, how they functioned, and what they meant. It is a story that will resonate across the generations. For those of us who learned to love the natural world and maybe learned a little about ourselves by grace of the Adirondack camp experience, this book will bring back a lot of memories.

PHILIP G. TERRIE

Preface

WHAT IS "CAMP"? The word has many meanings in the Adirondacks, from a bark lean-to with balsam branches covering the floor, to a palatial estate with dozens of buildings. One meaning, familiar to Adirondackers and outsiders as well, denotes a residential educational program for children that takes place in the summer.

"Sleepaway" camp, a uniquely American institution, was born in the Northeast. The Adirondack region, while not exactly the birthplace of camping, was an important nursery for the institution. In 1998, the Adirondack Museum began studying children's camps to learn more about the influence of the Adirondack environment on camping, the ways in which camping reflected trends in American society, and the impact of camping on the Adirondack economy. From 2003–2006 the museum mounted the exhibit A Paradise for Boys and Girls: Children's Camps in the Adirondacks. Out of research for that exhibit grew this book.

Our children's camp research produced a directory of 334 camps in the Adirondack Park and near environs. For some, we have only a single reference in a tourist guide. For others, we have collected brochures and photographs, reminiscences, letters, published histories, and artifacts. Some camps probably were open for only a few summers. Others have celebrated their centennials. One of these, Camp Dudley, is the oldest camp in the country still in operation. A few camps in the region were founded recently. We know that millions of children have attended these residential Adirondack camps, but we cannot tell just how many because of the incompleteness of the records. The attentive reader will notice that illustrations in this book do not always correspond exactly to the time period discussed in the text they accompany, but the activities they depict will. This discrepancy is not always because we lack photographs from the appropriate time period; in some cases we delib-erately chose pictures from another time to emphasize the traditional nature of children's camping in the region.

Today the phrase "happy camper" has entered the American vernacular, and Americans all over the country ship their kids off to day camp at the local YMCA, or to baseball camp at a college to learn pitching from a major leaguer. Adirondack camps have remained fairly traditional. While individual camps have added new activities such as ultimate Frisbee and updated their equipment with zip lines and jet skis, most Adirondack camp programs remain grounded in the natural world.

The Adirondack Museum is located at the center of the Adirondack Park, a vast mosaic of state and private land that constitutes the largest public park in the contiguous United States. Since 1894 nearly half the Adirondack Park's six million acres have been protected as "forever wild" by the New York State constitution. Addressing the changing face of the Adirondacks as a wilderness place is one of the central themes of the Adirondack Museum. Since the museum opened to the public in 1957, its exhibitions and publications have documented the complex interaction between people and the land, as well as cultural attitudes toward nature.

This exhibition and publication present for the first time in a popular format a focused look at the subject of Adirondack children's camps. We are indebted to the scholarship of consulting historians Leslie Paris and Joan Jacobs Brumberg, and museum curator Hallie Bond, who also served as exhibit curator. Museum staff and consultants worked with energy and commitment to bring this important study to the public.

DAVID L. PAMPERIN, Director, Adirondack Museum
CAROLINE M. WELSH, Chief Curator, Adirondack Museum

Acknowledgments

AS IN ANY PROJECT OF THIS SCOPE, the people named on the cover received a great deal of assistance of all kinds. The individuals and organizations named below are the ones who helped in large blocks. The project could not have reached this stage, however, without the innumerable small gifts—an e-mail recounting experiences at a camp of which I had been previously unaware, an envelope full of a child's letters from camp written sixty years ago, a story from a property owner about what he found when he purchased the place. We owe the givers of these gifts a great debt of gratitude.

When the museum began the children's camps project it engaged Leslie Paris, then a graduate student at the University of Michigan, as a consultant. She was working on her dissertation on children's camps in New York State between the world wars. The research report on Adirondack camps in that period that she wrote for the museum, the list of the camps she found, and the resources she located laid the foundation for the exhibit. Much of the discussion of camping between the wars in my essay is based on Paris's dissertation, "Children's Nature: Summer Camps in New York State, 1919–1941."

Cornell professor Joan Jacobs Brumberg was also a consultant to the exhibit and was extremely helpful in researching this book. Her suggestions for further research and her responses to questions went far beyond her consulting duties.

Adirondack Museum system administrator Michael Miller initiated me into the mysteries of data analysis and made possible several new ways of looking at the vast amount of camp information and photographs we gathered in the course of the project. Miller also masterminded the Camp Memory Project, the museum's first complex interactive computer program. At a computer station in the exhibit, and via the Internet, people can enter memories and information about camps in the region into our database. We have learned of a number of "new" camps this way and have collected the sort of personal impressions of camp unavailable in almost any other way.

As always, Mason Smith was patient in listening to my latest find, generous with moral support, and a great help with his suggestions for editing. Ann-Marie Carroll's infectious enthusiasm about camping in general and, of course, her camp in particular, and her belief in this project helped me keep up my enthusiasm.

The camps project has greatly increased the Adirondack Museum archives, and we now have available to researchers much more material on organized camping than we had when Dr. Paris began her research. I am grateful to the many people who heard about the Adirondack Museum's children's camps project and came forth with their treasured camp patches, scrapbooks, photos, and memories.

I would like to thank the following for opening their camp archives and for being particularly generous with their memories: John Leach of the Adirondack Woodcraft Camps, Karen G. Meltzer of the Brant Lake Camp, Ruth and Melvin Wortman of Camps Che-Na-Wah and Baco, Paul Grinwis at Camp Dudley, Naomi Levine of Camp Greylock, Frances McIntyre and Ann-Marie Carroll of Camp Jeanne d'Arc, Jack Swan of Camp Pok-O-Moonshine, Nancy Gucker Birdsall and Peter L. Gucker of the North Country Camps, Ed Lapidus of the Raquette Lake Camps, and Tad Welch of Tanager Lodge. The Schroon Lake Historical Society was a rich resource for Schroon Lake area camps. Richard Salomon, son of Julian

Harris Salomon, provided material from his father's archives that illuminated the use of Ernest Thompson Seton's Woodcraft ideas in children's camps.

My colleagues in the curatorial, library, and education departments should be recognized for all their work on the children's camps project in all its aspects—exhibit, programs, and book. I am grateful to former director Jacqueline Day for initiating the project, and to her successor, David Pamperin, for supporting the publication. The institutional advancement staff deserves thanks, as well, for finding funding for the project.

The Hirsch and Braine Raskin Foundation, whose generous financial support made possible both the exhibit and this book, is in a different category of assistance and one that is essential. We thank them.

HALLIE E. BOND

"A Paradise for Boys and Girls"

1 *"Pink Music"*

Continuity and Change at Early Adirondack Summer Camps[1]

SEVERAL YEARS AGO, I was sitting in the Camp Dudley archives looking through old memorabilia when I overheard a group of boys off in the distance, shouting in unison:

D-U-D-L-E-Y
White-washed cookies, chicken pie
Pink Music, pickerel fry
Westport! Westport!
My! oh, my!

I had never before heard these words spoken, but the cheer seemed oddly familiar to me nonetheless. Then I realized that I had seen the cheer written out in the pages of the camp's 1906 brochure. Evidently Dudley campers have been reciting it over the course of a century.[2]

Camp Dudley, the New York State Young Men's Christian Association (YMCA) camp, is the oldest extant children's camp in the nation. When it was founded in 1885 near Newburgh, New York, by YMCA volunteer Sumner F. Dudley, it was one of the first YMCA boys' camps, at a time when the national organization was just beginning to enter into "boys' work."[3] Summer camps were among the most successful of the organization's projects, as evidenced by the success of what Dudley and his boys first called "Camp Bald Head" (because the boys had very short haircuts). Over the next few years, Dudley and a small staff of men brought a growing number of boys from place to place, finally relocating to Lake Champlain near the Adirondack town of Westport in 1891. Dudley died in 1897, but the camp, after making one last move along the lake in 1908,

continued to thrive. Today's Dudleyites are well aware of their camp's heritage and they take their traditions seriously, passing them down with care from one generation to the next. The counselors are still called "leaders"; the campers are still assigned their own personal identification number (in ascending order from year to year) upon their arrival; and they still learn a camp cheer whose reference to "pink music" (a kind of pink lemonade, and a precursor to today's "bug juice") is most definitely out of date.

In the course of writing a book about the early history of American summer camps, I have had the pleasure of traveling through this mountainous region to visit camps, to talk with former campers and camp directors, and to look through memorabilia. The Adirondacks boast one of the oldest and largest summer camp clusters in the nation. Many camps have come and gone over the years, leaving few traces. Others have thrived, often in the same family, for generations. As a historian, I have sometimes had the sense of being in two places simultaneously: on the one hand, reading through the records of a distant past so rich in detail that it almost leaps off the printed page, and on the other, passing through camps where contemporary children continue to swim, canoe, and work on craft projects. When campers sing old songs around the evening campfire or recycle camp conventions that have been in use since before their own grandparents were born, these two worlds—the historical and the present-day—can overlap significantly, as they did for me while I pored over files that summer evening at Camp Dudley.

Hikers at Camp Dudley, ca. 1925. Courtesy of Camp Dudley, YMCA Inc.

Still, no camp culture is frozen in time. At Camp Dudley, for instance, many traditions have changed over the years. Some shifts in custom have reflected alterations to the physical landscape, as when cabins were built to replace the canvas tents. As American society was transformed, Camp Dudley changed as well. Before the Second World War, almost all YMCA camps around the country were racially segregated; today, photographs on the Dudley camp website pointedly showcase the community's racial diversity. Other customs slowly fell out of fashion; the Dudley expression "pickerel bait," which referred to a young, uninitiated camper back in the early twentieth century, is not in use today. New trends in recreation have emerged; in recent years, for instance, Dudley offerings have included a climbing wall and a ropes course.

Adirondack camps have always run a middle course between continuity and change. While they promise old-fashioned pleasures, they have also continually adapted to new ideas in children's recreation and in American culture at large. At every juncture, staff and campers have brought their own particular personalities and experiences into the mix, making each summer unique. Camp traditions have been vital to the Adirondack camp experience, but they are also constantly being invented, recycled, revisited, and sometimes let go.

In the late nineteenth century, the American men who founded the first summer camps were concerned about the rapidly changing world in which they lived. These men—most of them well-educated, native-born Protestants—acknowledged that they lived in an era of ingenuity and progress. But advanced civilization, they feared, posed important risks to their health and well-being. The industrial age seemed "artificial" as compared to an older rural culture; the busy pace of modern urban life was exhausting, the cities were noisy and dirty, an older cultural heritage was being eroded, and the comforts of civilization threatened to make well-to-do men "soft." Many of these men, so-called "muscular Christians," further argued that the church had promoted an overly passive, feminized brand of Christianity. Eager and idealistic, they earnestly discussed ways of improving their own physical and moral vitality.[4]

One oft-proposed solution to these many concerns

was camping in the outdoors. In the late nineteenth century, many middle- and upper-class Americans (who, unlike industrial workers and farmers, could afford the time and expense of such summer vacations) took up this back-to-nature idea with enthusiasm.[5] Many tourists first became aware of the particular allure of the Adirondacks upon reading Boston clergyman William H. H. "Adirondack" Murray's 1869 best-selling description of his camping trips, *Adventures in the Wilderness; or, Camp-Life in the Adirondacks.* As they rushed to the region, they claimed to have been inspired by the book's glowing descriptions of the area's natural beauty, and by Murray's testament to its positive effects upon his own vigor and health. In fact, so many tourists came, so quickly, to a region unequipped to provide them with adequate guides and hotels, that they were soon dubbed "Murray's Fools."[6]

By the 1870s, the local tourist economy had caught up to its urban vacationers' desires. Tourists wanted to commune with nature, but they also expected to do so in some comfort, and the Adirondack tourist industry was responsive to the whims of a wealthy elite. Families vacationed at lodges and fancy resorts where they could enjoy the lovely vistas around them by day and then consume eight-course meals at night. Some of the most affluent Americans purchased lavish country places, called "Great Camps," which combined the pleasures of luxurious estates with substantial privacy. "Muscular Christians" who sought more strenuous (but still comfortable) hunting and fishing expeditions hired local guides who knew the terrain, carried the provisions, set up camp, and made dinner each night.

In the 1870s and 1880s, a few men began to plan similar kinds of camping trips specifically for urban boys. These leaders hoped to develop something especially fitted to what they took to be the particular, age-specific needs of boys: vigorous physical activity to strengthen their bodies for the year to come; quiet time in settings of natural beauty to engage them in moral reflection; and adult leadership to better socialize them for future success. When Sumner Dudley first brought a small number of boys to camp for a week in 1885 near Newburgh, New York, his plan was typical of these early summer camp efforts. The days were spent in outdoor activities such as swimming, singing, and boating. At dusk, when Dudley gathered his campers together for prayer, he hoped to inspire in them a love of God as well as the natural world.[7]

By the turn of the twentieth century, the YMCA camp movement was booming nationwide. A few dozen private camps had also been founded from the late 1870s onward, many of them in New Hampshire and Maine.[8] In the Adirondacks, turn-of-the-century private boys' camps included Camp Rondack, Camp Rainbow, Camp So-High, and the more long-lived Camp Adirondack (founded in 1904 on Lake George by Dr. Elias Brown, who had previously worked as the Camp Dudley doctor), Penn (at Valcour, 1905), Pok-O-Moonshine (at Willsboro, 1906), and Riverdale (at Long Lake, 1912).[9] Their founders were often school principals and teachers—Charles Robinson of Camp Pok-O-Moonshine, for instance, was also the principal of Peekskill Academy in Peekskill, New York—and some of their first clients were their own students. Their camps tended to offer tutoring in schoolwork in addition to swimming, hiking, and nature study. Still, their leaders' focus was less on book learning than on health and character development, and they particularly emphasized the beneficial effects of a vacation in the woods. As Dr. and Mrs. Coit of Camp So-High promised their clients in 1906, "such a life is safe, sane and healthful."[10] Parents responded in kind. In a typical testimonial letter, one Pittsburgh father praised Camp Pok-O-Moonshine: "William returned from camp [in 1911] having gained fifteen pounds in about seven weeks. He was a perfect picture of health and I think the camp life not only built him up physically but had a good moral effect."[11]

From the beginning of the twentieth century onward, these boys' camps were joined by a smaller group of girls' camps, some of them founded by a new generation of college-educated women. The French Recreation Class for Girls on Lake Placid, possibly the first girls' camp in the Adirondack region, exemplified an emergent ideal of genteel female physicality. The campers, according to the 1896 brochure, participated in outdoor exercise, walking, and rowing (always "suitably accompanied"), daily French study, optional classes in botany and sketching, and special college preparatory courses.[12] As a more physically adventurous feminine ideal became the norm, increasing numbers of girls began to spend summers at such institutions as Camp Cedar (Pottersville, 1908), Black Elephant

Grand Central Station in New York City was the point of debarkation for campers headed for the Adirondacks. In this photo, about 1960, counselors from Echo Camp collect their charges before boarding the train. The Adirondack Museum.

(Lake George, 1910) and Boulder Point (Rainbow Lake, 1916).[13]

High mountains, quiet lakes, and the promise of virgin wilderness (however inaccurate in a region where logging, mining, and farming had driven the economy for generations) far from major cities: all of these gave Adirondack camps significant cachet. Adirondack camps were also generally rather expensive; in 1906, So-High cost $125 for the nine-week season, and in 1896, the French Recreation Camp cost between $225 and $300 for fourteen weeks. As a point of comparison, at the turn of the century the average annual wage of an unskilled worker in the northern United States was well under $500 per year.[14] Adirondack camp fees effectively kept the patronage limited to a monied elite.

In this sense, while Camp Dudley has become an icon of the Adirondack camping tradition, it was never entirely typical of area summer camps. In 1923, the cost of a Dudley season was $130 (plus return transportation and the cost of the camp uniform).[15] This was expensive by YMCA stan-

dards, but by Adirondack camp standards it was quite affordable. Private camps cost far more: as much as $400 per child during the heady years of the 1920s, and more than $300 during the leaner years of the Depression. In the interwar years, a few youth groups and charitable organizations founded Adirondack camps, but these were the exception, not the rule.[16] Nationally, the greatest boom in camping occurred in the market for moderately priced camps run by youth groups, which served a wide range of families. Most early Adirondack camp leaders did not aim to serve such diverse clienteles. "At Camp," a 1926 Schroon Lake Camp brochure argued, "the boy mingles with boys of his own age and standing; perhaps with boys of greater attainment and talent, boys who are born to lead."[17] For middle- and upper-class northeastern parents, selecting a camp was another means of declaring their own (and their children's) place in the social order.

In the early twentieth century, adults of all kinds became increasingly convinced that a stay at camp was a good, age-appropriate antidote to ten months of city life for boys and girls, rich and poor. By the 1930s, perhaps as many as 15 percent of American children (but a significantly higher percentage of white children from the urban northeast) attended a summer camp at least once.[18] In my research on early-twentieth-century Adirondack camps, I found evidence of only a handful of Latino and Asian American children, and no African Americans, who attended as campers.[19] White American parents had far more options: camps for boys, for girls, and a few for preadolescents of both sexes; camps for younger and older children; camps for Protestants, Catholics, and Jews. A number of early-twentieth-century Adirondack camps also offered a specialty of some kind: a focus on hiking at Camp Pok-O-Moonshine, for instance, or music at the Ruth Doing Music Camp (Chateaugay, 1925).

Perhaps the single most important dividing lines in Adirondack camping were religious and ethnic. Christian and Jewish campers circulated through separate leisure networks, only occasionally meeting at sports competitions or on hikes in the region. Ever since 1877, when Jewish financier Joseph Seligman had been publicly turned away from the Saratoga Springs Grand Union Hotel (just south of the Adirondacks) on account of his Jewishness, policies of anti-Semitic exclusion had become commonplace in many resort communities. Numerous Christian-led children's camps in the region, as part of their promise of exclusivity, promised that only "boys of good character from Christian families" would be accepted.[20] But although many rural communities were unfriendly to Jewish tourists, an important regional cluster of Jewish camps emerged, especially in the southeast Adirondacks. Schroon Lake Camp (Schroon Lake, 1906), the first private Jewish camp in all of New York State, was founded by Rabbi Isaac Moses, leader of a Reform congregation in New York City. The immediate success of his camp inspired similar efforts.[21] By the interwar years, the list of Jewish camps near or on Schroon Lake included Brant Lake, Cayuga, Idylwold, Nawita, Paradox, Pine Tree, Red Wing, Rondack, Ronwood, Severance, and Woodmere.[22]

This, then, was the world of early Adirondack summer camps—a world in which relatively privileged children spent up to two months away from home learning to swim, putting on circuses and water pageants, competing in base-

ball tournaments, and singing around the campfire at night. That this model was appealing to many directors, parents, and campers was evident by 1924, when Porter Sargent published his first *Handbook of Summer Camps,* an annual series that focused mainly on private camps. Sargent reported that "[a]lthough late in their beginnings, summer camps have so developed in the Adirondacks, that the region now takes rank with Sebago Lake, Lake Winnepesaukee [*sic*] and the Upper Connecticut Valley" [private camp-rich areas of Maine, New Hampshire, and Vermont, respectively].[23] Another sign of the region's prominence was that Adirondack camp directors often played active roles in directors' associations: Elias Brown of Camp Adirondack, Herman Beckman of Camp Dudley, and Frank Hackett of Camp Riverdale all served terms as directors of the national camping organization, while other Adirondack camp leaders were regular contributors to industry journals. Adirondack camps were very well known, whether or not they were the most typical of national trends.

To what degree were Adirondack camps unique? Generally speaking, elite camps were more likely than others to be located far from major cities, to offer expensive activities such as riding or sailing, to provide a higher ratio of staff to campers, and to have special camp uniforms (in the first few decades of the twentieth century, girls at Adirondack camps often wore middy-style shirts and bloomers, and boys wore shirts and shorts; both outfits were usually accessorized with sweaters and kerchiefs in the camp colors, or else emblazoned with the camp's initials). All of these differences gave Adirondack camps a particular cachet. But the camp experience was shaped here, as elsewhere, by a national camp culture that transcended regional, religious, and class differences. After all, some campers were clients of different camps from year to year, children and staff discussed their camp experiences with one another during the school year, and prominent camp directors wrote up their ideas in industry journals such as *Camping Magazine* and *Camp Life.* In all these ways, popular ideas migrated from camp to camp and from one region to another.

Of what did these traditions consist? The Adirondack camp season began when children set off to camp, usually by train or ferry. This trip was exciting for some, dreadful for others. For a homesick boy traveling to Adirondack

Bugler at Camp Che-Na-Wah, ca. 1930. Courtesy of Ruth and Melvin Wortman, Camps Che-Na-Wah and Baco.

GIRL SCOUT CAMP EAGLE ISLAND, 2004

Beside the friendships I made, what remains with me the most is the entire camp culture that includes so much more than one isolated memory. EIC is a place that is steeped in tradition, that Girl Scouts over the years have treasured and preserved in place. It includes the physical landscape and all its "furniture" like the heavy canoe paddles painted with fanciful designs, the mess hall plaques for each summer with counselor's names made in match sticks, a quote from a song and a beautiful painting, the interiors—the mounted heads on the walls, the birchbark plaque detailing which units hiked which Adirondack peak, all the original buildings. Even the waterfront maintains its original appearance. It's also the intangibles—the place names (Green Johns, Mariner's Rock), the pranks, the singing at every meal and at every opportunity, Song Contest, the rivalries between units, the camp food.[51]

Woodcraft Camps in 1939, the voyage was hardly propitious: "I was not the most enthusiastic twelve-year old," William Steckel would later recall, and "the ride to camp was wet and gloomy for the 'new boys.' "[24] Returning campers who were reuniting with old friends were often much merrier—so much so that their counselors had trouble getting them to sleep on the overnight train trip into the mountains. After trips of up to twenty-four hours, children felt that they had traveled far from their ordinary lives by the time they arrived at camp.[25]

As they settled in, early-twentieth-century campers were initiated into fairly predictable daily routines. They awoke to the sound of a bugle or bell. Some were required to perform "setting-up" exercises (calisthenics) on the lawn or to take a quick dip in the lake before sitting down to eat

their breakfast at communal tables. The food tended toward the plain and predictable: eggs, oatmeal, or pancakes for breakfast; stew, macaroni, or hot soup at lunch; meat and potatoes for dinner. After finishing their first meal of the day, the campers gathered for news and the raising of the American flag, and went off to clean their tents or cabins for inspection. They then participated in a series of athletic activities—water sports such as swimming (often twice daily), canoeing, rowing, and sailing; land sports such as baseball, basketball, volleyball, tennis, and sometimes riding or archery—made crafts, and rehearsed for upcoming plays and pageants. To keep up with this active pace, the campers spent the "rest hour" after lunch sleeping, writing letters, or quietly reading. After dinner and the lowering of the flag, they enjoyed a range of evening activities including plays, movies, and campfires. This routine was punctuated by special events, including camp circuses and Indian pageants; overnight hikes and (as campers gained in skill) days-long canoe trips; inter-camp swimming meets and baseball games; and occasional dances with boys or girls from neighboring camps.

Many insider rituals incorporated campers into a welcoming community. At Camp Severance, the girls took on such nicknames as Peanut, Bo, Noodles, Frenchie, Miggy, and Cricket, and learned to call their counselors Fuzzy, Sunny, Petie, Brownie, and Horsey.[26] These new names ritualized innovative ways of thinking about family and kinship outside of traditional bounds; at many camps, counselors became "Aunt" or "Uncle," while the youngest children were under the care of a "Camp Mother."

Structured competition, on the other hand, acknowledged that camper loyalties were often smaller than the camp as a whole. Among the most popular of these more competitive events (except at self-consciously noncompetitive camps) was Color War, which ritually divided the camp into two factions. At Brant Lake Camp, the Color War festivities began on "Tap Day," when every new boy was assigned to either the Green or the Gray team (and would remain a Green or a Gray for as long as he returned to camp). Days of competition followed, not only in athletics but also in checkers, fishing, and art, guaranteeing that every Brant Lake boy, even the least athletically gifted, might help his team.[27] Color War made room, however limited, for camper aggression: at Camp Rondack, where each girl was either a Ron or a Dack, the Dack team of 1936 was not unusual in promising to "drop a battle-axe on Ron Team's head."[28] At the end of Color War, the hatchets were literally and symbolically reburied.

Camp pranks similarly conjoined community and competition. At many boys' camps, new campers were sent out to hunt snipe, a kind of waterfowl, and told to bring the catch back to camp for dinner. But as every experienced camper already knew, these boys were heading off on a literal wild-goose chase. If they returned to camp another year, then they too would have a laugh at the expense of the new boys.[29] At Camp Dudley, experienced campers sent the "greenhorns" off to look for "dark mikalos" (the name actually derived from a Dudley initiation ceremony, not an object or animal), striped paint, square tent peg holes, and a stocking to fit a leg of lamb.[30] "Pie-ing" (or short-sheeting) other campers' beds was another common summer camp ritual. After a group of Camp Che-Na-Wah girls found their beds pied one night, they returned the favor; as their camp newspaper later reported, " 'Revenge is mine' saith Bunk 12."[31]

Much of what I have just described as central to Adirondack camp culture will be recognizable to those who have attended camps in other regions of the United States. So too, Native American iconography and legends were im-

Campers from Tanager Lodge on a peak near the Chateaugay Lakes; most of the peaks in this area are trailless and require map and compass work to ascend. Courtesy of Tanager Lodge.

portant to most American camps. From the beginning of the twentieth century onward, many camp leaders were inspired by Ernest Thompson Seton's Woodcraft Indians (an organization founded in 1901 and later renamed the Woodcraft League), and by Seton's versions of Native American rituals such as the Council Fire and the Omaha Tribal Greeting.[32] Many campers found these rites deeply moving and adventurous; as one former Adirondack Woodcraft camper would later recall, it was thrilling "hearing one's name called from the four points of the compass and then having to pull the blanket tight around you and with heart pounding walk out into the night."[33] Yet if Seton and his followers aimed to express reverence for Indians' connection to nature, the nostalgia of "woodcraft" also painted Native peoples as premodern (and in the modern world, as either disappeared or doomed). Because "woodcraft" drew on the traditions of tribes across the continent, it tended to offer more of a smorgasbord of elements—a tepee here, a totem pole there—than an accurate reenactment of local Native traditions. Further, especially at boys' camps, "playing Indian" was often a pretext for exploring boys' so-called "primitive" instincts. "This Indian Village gives the boy the much needed opportunity to express his inherent savagery. Just to be free, to run, to climb, to shout and yell like a wild Indian on a war-path!" as the 1928 Camp Ticonderoga brochure explained.[34]

Some Adirondack camp activities lent themselves to a more specific appreciation of the region. On road trips away from camp, campers learned about sites of historical interest such as the Revolutionary War-era Fort Ticonderoga, traveled to spaces of natural beauty such as the strange rock formations of Ausable Chasm, and toured Lake George as tourists. Hardy campers canoed the lakes and hiked the high mountains; each summer, for instance, a highlight of the Pok-O-Moonshine season was the climb up Mount Marcy.[35] And each camp had its own special places, little known to guidebooks but important to that camp's lore. The Camp Riverdale boys, for example, frequently hiked to a place in the Cold River they called "Nymph's Bathtub," where they could sit in a cleft between two rock walls with their shoulders immersed in icy water flowing down the rocks from above.[36] One young Riverdale camper of 1942 wrote for many when he praised the "over nyghts" and "hicks" that had brought him into other parts

of the Adirondack Park.[37] In later years, former campers would fondly recall the mountains and lakes where they had enjoyed these early adventures.

Finally, after eight or nine weeks of swimming, hiking, and yelling camp cheers, children prepared to return home. On the last evening of the summer season, they participated in a special communal ritual: a lavish banquet and awards ceremony. At Schroon Lake Camp one year, the boys feasted on raw vegetables and pickles, grapefruit, broiled salmon, "parisienne" potatoes, dinner rolls, consommé, roast stuffed chicken, string beans, corn on the cob, candied sweet potatoes, Waldorf salad, vanilla ice cream with chocolate sauce, fresh fruit, stuffed dates, cake, and after-dinner mints: a meal that returned them, at least metaphorically, to civilization.[38]

As children grew more comfortable at camp, they be-

Photography was encouraged by Ernest Thompson Seton as an aid to nature observation. Some camps, such as Eagle Cove, seen here in a 1950 promotional shot, had their own darkrooms that fostered creativity as well as provided results for the budding photographers working far from commercial photo processing. Courtesy of Joan Jacobs Brumberg.

Like many Progressive-era camps, Camp Lincoln had a nature study program in which campers learned identification of plants and animals through direct observation in the 1920s. Courtesy of North Country Camps.

came invested in these various customs. Those who returned another summer would know all about "dark mikalos" or "Tap Day." They would be able to sing the old camp songs, they could look forward to the camp fair and the water pageant, and they could hope to avenge the past year's team loss in Color War. For all of these reasons, children were often keen proponents of camp traditions. Still, camp culture was always in flux, at least to some degree. To take one example, most camp leaders made little of Native American iconography until Seton fired their imaginations. At Camp Dudley, the annual Indian pageant that grew to be an important camp tradition by the 1920s, drawing hundreds of spectators, didn't exist before 1914.[39] Some camp leaders tried out Indian campfires for a few years, eliminated them, and then reincorporated them. Much could change over the course of a few years, as staff changed and as one cohort of campers aged out of camp and another took its place.

Sometimes camp traditions gave way to broader changes in American culture. Weekly chapel talks would re-

main a highlight of Dudley life, but Bible study would decrease in importance over the years: a reflection of the increased secularization of American culture and of the decline of "muscular Christianity" after the First World War. In the first two decades of the century, some camp leaders prided themselves on their highly organized schedules and systems of badges and awards, seeing in these the most effective and "scientific" means of disciplining children. In the interwar years, increasing numbers of self-styled "progressive" camp directors, influenced by philosopher John Dewey and his call for child-centered "progressive education," turned away from these kinds of incentives. The directors of Camp Lincoln and Camp Whippoorwill (1920 and 1931, Keeseville) promised "greater chance for adventure, and a let-down from the competitive drive and scheduled routine of the usual school day."[40] At Camp Treetops (Lake Placid, 1920), children lived apart from their counselors, to promote independence; they had no camp store, to promote equality amongst them; and their daily program was self-directed, to encourage them to take more initiative.[41] By the early 1930s, awards and sports competitions were somewhat deemphasized at Camp Dudley as well.[42]

The ongoing transformation of summer camp culture was particularly obvious at those moments when the facilities underwent expansion. Although the first Adirondack camps were prestigious, and a few were built on the site of old Great Camps and resorts, most had rather humble beginnings: tents for the ten or twenty children, a large wooden building in which to eat and play games on rainy days, a field for sports, and a lake in which to swim. As they gained clients, elite camps' leaders quickly expanded their offerings; by 1906 at Camp So-High, for instance, the campers had access to a darkroom for photographic work, a tennis court, and a library.[43] Although camps were organized as alternatives to "civilization," their leaders often measured their success through the expansion of their own physical plants.

Some changes to the traditional architecture of camp life were more controversial than others. In the 1930s at Camp Dudley, the wooden cabins that are still in use today gradually replaced tents. This particular upgrade occasioned a fair amount of criticism within the camp community precisely because it appeared to tread on a cherished camp legacy. For experienced Dudleyites, tents were an integral part of camp life: living closer to nature but protected from the elements. "We never had the feeling that we were roughing it," a camper of the 1920s later reported. "It was wonderful to feel the cool—sometimes cold—night air flowing over you when the tent flaps were up. We were snug as could be sleeping between the folds of a warm quilt kept tightly in place by a wool blanket stretched across us and tucked under the two by fours that held the canvas bottom of our two-decker bunks."[44] Still, tents required constant attention: rips in the canvas had to be repaired, ropes carefully loosened during thunderstorms, and the skunks that lived under the wooden platforms gently encouraged to depart.[45] Tents were also vulnerable to high spirits; for one tent group to loosen or cut the guy ropes of another group's tent was a favorite camp prank.

Cabins promised less trouble. They did not require constant repair, did not have to be carefully dried and put away at the end of the season, better sheltered campers from the elements, and were cheaper over the long run than tents, which had to be replaced at regular intervals. Yet when the first three wooden cabins were built, the camp newspaper, the *Dudley Doings*, reported that "many of the oldtimers are a bit skeptical, they are being convinced of the value of these additions."[46] Cabins, many alumni felt, were "soft" and not "real camping." Still, many campers

Camp Dudley campus, ca. 1920. Courtesy of Camp Dudley, YMCA Inc.

Cottage interior, Camp Dudley, ca. 1930. Courtesy of Camp Dudley, YMCA Inc.

soon saw their benefits. As one boy later recalled, "some of us resisted the idea of building cabins. That, we felt, would mean we were no longer camping, and in a sense that was true." But, he continued, "I'll have to admit, though, that the summer when the first three cabins were available, and my tent was one of the nine which each had three weeks in a cabin, and our turn coincided with three weeks of almost continuous rain, I weakened a bit."[47]

Not all camps would go this route. Boy Scout and Girl Scout camp leaders continued to value "primitive camping" on ideological grounds, and at a number of such camps children continued to live in tents and even to do some of their own cooking. But the leaders of organization-run camps did not face the same pressures as did directors of private camps to offer new and improved facilities. Nor did most youth groups' camps have alumni as dedicated and financially generous as those at Camp Dudley, who collectively organized one building campaign after the next.

When I traveled in the Adirondacks, one camp stood out in my mind as having changed the least since its early days: Tanager Lodge, a coeducational camp founded on Upper Chateaugay Lake in 1925 by forester and camp consultant Fay Welch. Welch had a long history in the region, where he had camped as a boy and worked as a guide before joining the faculty of Syracuse University's College of Forestry and becoming a consultant to the Girl Scouts and Boy Scouts. Welch shunned such modern camp conveniences as electricity, flush toilets, hot showers, and wooden cabins, and his campers used kerosene lanterns and bathed

in the lake.[48] In the 1920s, this rusticity was common, especially for a "progressive" camp influenced by the call to simplicity. Today, however, the camp is exceptional in having remained quite true to this earlier vision. Perhaps its small size—about fifty campers—has facilitated the maintenance of tradition, given that camp leaders often updated their facilities as they admitted greater numbers of children. In today's diverse camp market, where every camp aims to offer something unique, Tanager Lodge serves clients, some of them the grandchildren of former campers, who actively seek out a simpler experience.

But perhaps less traditional summer camps are authentically "camp-y" in their own way for attempting to celebrate "progress" as much as tradition. The Dudley cabin campaign, with its overt shift in the camp landscape, showed how new impulses could be reconciled with venerable custom. After all, the fuss over cabins actually settled down quite quickly, evidence of the speed with which new camp traditions could be forged and old ones laid aside. Even if Dudley was an old and established camp, the aver-

Morning assembly, Tanager Lodge, 1990. Courtesy of Tanager Lodge.

age camper attended for only a few years. What might seem like apostasy to one generation of campers would feel comfortable and familiar to campers only a few years later. One cohort's tradition would become another's legend about the "good old days."

Camp nostalgia is a complicated thing. "I suppose," noted one Camp Pok-O-Moonshine alumnus of the 1910s, "that every boy or master who has ever been at Pok-O is sure that the happy days he spent there really represent the camp's golden age."[49] At the oldest area camps, many aspects of camp culture have changed little over the past century, but each group of campers has experienced a slightly different camp. Some traditions have stood the test of time, others have not. If Sumner Dudley could see the camp that bears his name today, there is much that he would not recognize. But he would surely identify with the ambitions of today's camp leaders to provide children beneficial, healthful, and happy vacations in settings of striking loveliness.

2 "A Paradise for Boys and Girls"

Children's Camps in the Adirondacks

CAMP RIVERDALE sat on the western shore of Long Lake, in the center of the Adirondack Mountains. Standing on the beach as the sun came up across the lake, a boy in the summer of 1932 could look to his left and see the sun catch the tops of the trailless Santanoni Range. To his right, an island covered with white pine trees in the middle distance was overshadowed by the forested bulk of Kempshall Mountain. Across the lake, he knew, was a small farm where his morning milk came from, but in spite of this he could easily pretend he was the only person on the lake. He might even imagine that he was the first person ever to admire the scene.

CAMP RIVERDALE, 1932

This square mile of wooded land stretching back from a mile and a half of lake front, is a paradise for boys. Beauty reigns everywhere. . . . Nature rarely affords an outlook more inspiring. The surrounding woods with an infinite variety of forest life, are a constant source of wonder and of learning.[51]

Counselors and campers of Chippewa bunk, Camp Eagle Cove, 1952. Courtesy of Joan Jacobs Brumberg.

13

Scouts and leaders, Camp Russell, 1957. Courtesy of Alan Woodruff, Camp Russell.

In fact, the boy rising early might have been one of a community of sixty boys who had come to live in the woods for two months to learn skills their parents felt could only be learned in the woods. With the boys lived fifteen adults. Most of them were engaged in trying to teach the boys those skills—how to paddle a canoe, how to identify a white pine, and how to live together. They called their community a "camp" to highlight the fact that it was a temporary home in the woods.

As alone as it seemed to be, Camp Riverdale was one of many such communities across the Northeast and across the past century. In the Adirondacks alone, 336 residential children's camps have been founded. Most, like Riverdale, have closed. Seventy remain open, however, continuing the tradition of what has been called "the most important step in education that America has given the world." [1] Some of these camps were private enterprises intended to support the owners; some were run by youth organizations to teach

the organization's values. All were shaped by the educational theories of their day; by the concerns, conditions, and affluence of American society; and by the Adirondack environment. The story of organized camping in the Adirondacks is not only the story of millions of children discovering nature and themselves, but the story of the enduring influence of the Adirondack wilderness on a human institution.

"The Ministry of the Sun"

Before the Civil War, "city folk" visited the Adirondack region to counter the undesirable aspects of urban life. This vast area of seemingly untouched forests, mountains, and lakes provided a natural, calm retreat from the increasingly impersonal, grimy, fast-paced cities. These antebellum tourists, usually men and usually with a higher-than-average income, spent a month or two in the woods, hunting, fishing, and camping out in the company of local men who acted as guides.

After the Civil War, the Northeast experienced a period of unprecedented prosperity. The middle class not only got vacation time, but people like bank managers and store clerks now earned enough money to take themselves—and their families—out of town for that vacation. They also had a book that told them exactly how to get to "the woods": William Henry Harrison Murray's *Adventures in the Wilderness; or, Camp-life in the Adirondacks,* which was

---

"ADIRONDACK" MURRAY, CA. 1880

You can't grow strong trees under a glass roof. No more can you grow boys into strong men by any indoor culture. They need the freedom of the fields and the streams. They must breathe of the strength of the wind. They must receive through the pores of their skin the ministry of the sun. [52]

The Lake View House, Bolton, on Lake George, 1889. Photograph by Seneca Ray Stoddard. The Adirondack Museum, P29957.

published in 1869. Murray did not invent the idea that the Adirondack wilderness could rejuvenate a soul exhausted by the stress of life in a city, but he articulated it for the masses.[2]

Thanks in part to publicity such as Murray's book, the Adirondack region became extremely popular, a "Central Park for the World."[3] As Murray enticingly described, you could leave Boston at eight a.m. and be in Saranac Lake by five the next evening, your steamboat and stage having passed through "some of the sublimest scenery in the world" en route. Once in the woods you could camp out in a lean-to or a tent. If you were not inclined to "rough it" you could rely on a wide variety of accommodations, from Paul Smith's establishment on St. Regis Lake, the "St. James of the Wilderness,"[4] to small boarding houses or the extra room or hayloft of an enterprising settler. People continued to visit the region for hunting and fishing, but other, more sedentary outdoor pursuits such as golf, tennis, sightseeing, and botanizing became increasingly popular.

In the summer of 1891 a medical equipment salesman named Sumner F. Dudley took a group of boys from the Boy's Camping Society on a trip to Lake Champlain in search of much the same sort of respite from the city that

Murray's followers sought. The Boy's Camping Society had grown out of a week-long trip with seven boys that Dudley had taken six years before at the suggestion of the general secretary of the Newburgh Young Men's Christian Association. Nearly two hundred boys went on the trip to Lake Champlain, and they stayed for four weeks, living in tents, swimming, fishing, boating, and studying the Bible. In 1908 the YMCA purchased a permanent camp site on Barber's Point south of Westport for its camp for boys.[5] After Dudley's early death in 1897, the camp was named in his honor. It continues to this day, the oldest continuously operating children's camp in the country.

Dudley's camping trip was a somewhat unusual venture, but not a pioneering one. In 1881, Ernest Balch had opened his Camp Chocorua in New Hampshire. Although there were a few earlier children's camps, Camp Chocorua was enormously influential because of the publicity it received—most of it sought by Balch himself in an attempt to make his profit-making venture fly. He encouraged tourists to visit (one hundred watched the camp sports day in 1885), and Balch's sister and brother wrote two widely read articles published in the magazines *St. Nicholas* and *McClure's.*[6]

"A Tent Family, Camp Dudley." Courtesy of Camp Dudley, YMCA Inc.

Sumner Dudley was an amateur in the emerging field of child study and education, but he shared with the professionals a deep concern for the future of America's youth— and by the term "youth" he and the others meant boys. Late-nineteenth-century educators were very concerned about America's place in the world. Many of them felt that America's boys were getting too soft. American men were losing the supposed character of the pioneers that had made the country great. They had lost the hardiness, self-reliance, and close relationship with that defining trait of American culture, the wild outdoors. America was rapidly becoming the most powerful and prosperous nation on earth, and the educators wanted to keep it that way. Organized camps where children were gathered together in isolated communities with educators who were with them twenty-four hours a day, seven days a week, appealed greatly to youth workers because they were ideal places for character education.

Parents found the camp idea attractive too. They not only worried about their boys spending their summers with unsuitable companions and wasting time, but about the very real "dust, dirt, and dangers" of the cities.[7] In addition to the slums, crime, pollution, and tuberculosis that had been driving adults out of the cities for a generation, there seemed to be particular dangers for children. Epidemics of childhood disease such as diphtheria and scarlet fever recurred with alarming frequency in the cities, often hitting the young disproportionately. Infantile paralysis, or polio, seemed worst among city children in the summer.

The idea of sending children away for a summer of healthy outdoor living, without their parents but in the company of educators, proved attractive to several different groups. In the decade following Dudley's first trip to the Adirondacks, the foundations of organized camping were laid on the belief in character education and the importance of being close to nature. Not-for-profit, religion-based organizations such as the YMCA and profit-making educational ventures such as private schools pioneered camping in the Adirondacks. Between the establishment of Dudley's first camp on Lake Champlain in 1891 and 1910, seventeen more camps sprang up in the Adirondacks. Most

---

ADIRONDACK CAMP, 1906

Observe the boy at even a first-class summer hotel. There may be something for him to do much of the time, but what does he learn, and how is he better at the end of the summer? And what of the time when there is nothing special to do? Perhaps these hours are spent with the caddies or around the stable, or perhaps they are simply wasted.[53]

Young vacationers at the entrance to the Adirondack Mountain Reserve, St. Hubert's Inn in the distance, 1891. It was an idle summer vacation at this sort of hotel that early camp leaders were trying to replace. The Adirondack Museum, P15184.

were for Christian boys, but educators of girls and educators of Jewish boys soon adopted the idea of isolating a group of children in the woods for learning and health.

The YMCA founded Camp Dudley, and it inspired another early Adirondack camp that is also still in business. In 1900, George F. "Pop" Tibbitts founded Camp Iroquois on Lake George, a family camp that had a separate division for young men. Tibbitts, who worked as a YMCA administrator for thirty years, also established the Gospel Volunteers of the World to encourage daily devotional Bible study and personal evangelism. Camp Iroquois was meant to be "a spot where young people could spend a portion of their summer vacation in a Christian environment, along with healthful and picturesque surroundings."[8]

The Catholic Church was also a pioneer in organized camping. The College Camp was held on the grounds of the Catholic Summer School, a chautauqua-like institution founded in 1897 at Cliff Haven, just south of Plattsburgh. It was "simply a camp in the woods . . . where college boys may spend the summer vacation pleasantly, healthfully and safely."[9] By 1914 boys twelve and under were attending. Campers could go swimming, boating, fishing, bicycling, and canoeing; they could play golf, baseball, or tennis; and they could be tutored in academic subjects to prepare for the next school year.

Camps that were primarily profit-making ventures shortly followed the religion-based camps. Several of these either were summer sessions of private schools or were founded by headmasters or teachers in private schools. These educators not only had the entire summer off, but in Frank Sutliff Hackett's words, wondered "how to make a sound and profitable use of the long summer holiday."[10] Hackett, founder of both the Riverdale School in the Bronx

---

ADIRONDACK CAMP, 1906

The boys will learn the signs of the woods, trail following, camp making, cooking, and how to take care of themselves. These experiences are greatly enjoyed, and are invaluable in developing character and ability to get along.[54]

Campers and leaders at the College Camp at Cliff Haven on Lake Champlain, about 1905. Courtesy of Gordon W. Whigham Jr.

and Camp Riverdale on Long Lake, didn't clarify whether he meant "profitable" for himself and the faculty or for the students. Probably he meant both. Practical considerations—as well as an easily located potential clientele—also influenced the foundation of a number of camps by directors of private schools. These educators wanted to continue their educational programs throughout the year, and many had students who needed a place to go in the summer.

Meenahga Lodge, the earliest school-related camp, was the northern campus of the Adirondack-Florida School. In 1903 students began spending the fall and spring terms on Clear Pond, studying in the mornings and hiking, boating, and playing sports in the afternoons. By the end of the fall term, they could clear the lake of snow and play ice hockey.[11] Charles Alexander Robinson, headmaster of the Peekskill Military Academy, founded Camp Pok-O-Moonshine in 1905 near Willsboro in part to provide a place for his Latin American students to spend the long vacation. In 1912 alone, three private schools—Kent, Riverdale, and Taft—opened camps in the Adirondacks that remained open for ten to fifty years. The "academic" branch of Adirondack camping continued to grow. Seven more camps that were run by private schools or by the faculty of private schools were established between 1913 and 1929.

These early children's camps were novel institutions on

the Adirondack summer scene in that the guests were all children without their parents, but in some ways life at camp was similar to life at the region's resorts. Most of the camps had guides—local men who took the boys on hikes and canoe trips. The guide's pathfinding abilities were not essential to camp life, but his woodcraft—his ability to live comfortably in the wilderness—was an important part of the experience. A Mr. Pooler, the guide at the Adirondack

Staff at Camp Pok-O-Moonshine, 1905. Founder Charles Alexander Robinson sits in the center of the front row. Courtesy of Camp Pok-O-Moonshine.

"Old Eagle Eye" was George Sauseville, guide to the boys at Camp Dudley in the 1890s. Courtesy of Camp Dudley, YMCA Inc.

Camp (Lake George), was in charge of teaching woodcraft and campcraft to the boys when it opened. Guide Matthew Ryan lived on the property of Camp Pok-O-Moonshine— the camp property was purchased from him—and he provided many services, including maintenance of camp buildings and carrying the boys in his hay wagon on trips away from camp.

Plenty of fresh mountain air, rich in health-giving "balsamic vapors" and ozone, was one of the great attractions of the Adirondacks, for adults and for children. Fresh air was good for general health and also paramount in the prevention and treatment of tuberculosis.[12] Some camps also claimed to be free from ragweed and pollens in the hopes of attracting asthma and hay-fever sufferers.

Camp sleeping accommodations have always had plenty of fresh air. Tents were standard at most early

This postcard view of the Herkimer County YMCA camp on Fourth Lake documents the platform tents common to most early camps. Courtesy of Edward Comstock Jr.

Tents with wooden floors could be furnished with all the comforts of home, as at Camp Pok-O-Moonshine in 1910. This photograph appeared in the camp catalog, perhaps to reassure parents concerned that camp life would be too rough. Courtesy of Camp Pok-O-Moonshine.

Adirondack camps because of their openness; they were also traditional for "camping out," and they were cheap. They were also portable, an important consideration for camps that moved around or rented space before acquiring a permanent site. Tents also helped distinguish the summer home-at-camp from the children's homes in the cities.[13] At Pok-O-Moonshine the tents had heating stoves, chairs, dressing tables, and beds with wire spring mattresses. Accommodations at Camp Dudley were more rustic; tents there didn't have floors and campers slept on the ground,

POK-O-MOONSHINE, 1914

Just imagine having been out all afternoon exercising and coming home hungry as a bear to find buckwheat cakes and real maple syrup on the bill-of-fare. Not any of your hotel pancakes but as large as a plate and all you can eat. How fat one does get! Three good meals a day (supper is almost like dinner), with crackers and milk before bedtime— why, by the end of the summer you can't find your ribs and only believe in such things from hearsay. One boy gained thirty-five pounds in the nine weeks, but it was easy to put it on him, for he was tall and when spread over him it only amounted to about a half-inch deep. If you are short you may not gain more than twenty or even fifteen pounds.[S5]

POK-O-MACCREADY, 1916

There's a camp called Pok-O-MacCready
And it's a camp we all love.
Where the sun is always shining in the skies above.
There is swimming, fishing, hiking,
And it is all like a dream
But the thing we like the best of all
Is James's ice cream.[56]

protected by rubber blankets and "heavy comfortables," until after 1905.[14]

The abundance and quality of food were important selling points. Child mortality was a real threat around the turn of the twentieth century, and skinny children might be sick children. Camp was the time to build up the body of the city child so he would be better able to survive the school year. Regular meals were supplemented if necessary; the boys at Pok-O-Moonshine were served milk and crackers every night before bedtime, a ritual that was to appear at many Adirondack camps.[15]

At some of these early camps dining was more like eating at a resort than "camping out." At Cliff Haven, the campers "live in tents, like soldiers, dine at a first-class restaurant, unlike soldiers . . ."[16] The campers at Pok-O-Moonshine had James Hankins as chef for forty-seven years. Like the camp director, Hankins worked the rest of the year at the Peekskill Military Academy. Hankins has been dead for years, but campers still talk about his ice cream, made in a thirty-quart freezer. He hitched up a team and hauled the freezer to the foot of Pok-O-Moonshine Mountain to finish off the annual Poko Picnic of steak and potatoes—hardly a meal for "roughing it."[17]

Sports—particularly baseball but also tennis, basketball, and even ice hockey and water polo—were fixtures of organized camp life from its beginnings, even though one of the main purposes of coming to the Adirondacks was to get away from civilization and its trappings. The boys at Pok-O-Moonshine were assigned to their camp baseball team the day after they arrived, and the baseball series lasted throughout the summer. Games did have their rustic character, however. "The only hazard on using the baseball field," reminisced an early camper, "was the fact that it was

James Hankins and his colleague Jim, shown here ca. 1910, were both cooks at Camp Pok-O-Moonshine; they also cooked at the Peekskill Military Academy during the school year. Courtesy of Camp Pok-O-Moonshine.

Baseball at Camp Dudley, ca. 1920. Courtesy of Camp Dudley, YMCA Inc.

Basketball and tennis at Camp Naomi near Pottersville, 1925. The Adirondack Museum.

also the cow pasture. You had to be very careful when you slid onto second base."[18]

Basketball was wildly popular around the turn of the century in cities, and it became a fixture of camp life almost as soon as it was developed. The game was invented at the YMCA training college in Springfield, Massachusetts, in 1891, so it is perhaps not surprising to see it spread rapidly to the camping world where the YMCA was a pioneer. One of basketball's inventors, Luther Gulick, promoted team sports for their value in building character because they

Football team at Camp Pok-O-Moonshine, 1925. Courtesy of Camp Pok-O-Moonshine.

CAMP RIVERDALE, 1937

Indeed, the chief principle of Camp Riverdale is to give a boy during this brief summer interlude in the wilderness, a chance to be his best, to cultivate in a leisurely way those interests and skills which often lie dormant throughout the school year, to learn to love the quiet and the solitude of woods and mountains, and to live considerately and pleasantly with his fellows. Such an experience forms a life means of recuperation.[S7]

taught the importance of following rules, striving for symbolic rewards, and, of course, cooperation.[19] The popularity of team sports at colleges probably accounts for their popularity at the camps associated with schools. The camp football teams at Pok-O-Moonshine were named after college teams in the 1920s (Princeton, Navy, and Cornell) but the baseball teams were named after professional teams in the National and American Leagues.[20]

"A Brief Summer Interlude in the Wilderness"

The Adirondack Museum historic photo collection contains a fat album full of pictures that once belonged to Carrie Sinn, director of Camp Severance on Paradox Lake. In it is a group portrait of adults sitting on a rock wall, and they are all identified. The casual researcher would be tempted to flip past it for more engaging images, but it repays closer examination for it is figuratively if not literally a snapshot of camping philosophy in the period in which organized camping became an Adirondack institution. The picture was taken in 1927 at a camp leadership course.[21] At the time, camping was growing vigorously from its roots in character education, the back-to-nature movement, and private schools. The individuals in Carrie Sinn's picture represent the next development, a remarkable conjunction between the Progressive Education movement and a now almost-forgotten youth movement called the Woodcraft Indians. These men and women represent those who melded Progressivism and Woodcraft and established children's camps as educational institutions of a special sort, based on nature

Camp Leadership Course, 1927. Left to right (standing): Charles F. Smith, Mrs. W. Vinal, Bill Wessel, William Vinal, name unknown, Fay Welch. Left to right (sitting): Julian Harris Salomon, Ruby Joliffe, Florence Heinz, Carrie Sinn, Elbert K. Fretwell, Eleanor Deming, Agathe Deming, Margaret Protz, Lawrence Palmer (?), Wilford Allen, M.D. The Adirondack Museum, P53821.

Carrie Sinn's caption for this scrapbook photo was "Leatherwork with Southworth." The class was part of the Camp Leadership Course she attended in 1927. The Adirondack Museum, P52808.

study, camp-making skills, wilderness travel, manual training, sports, water skills, and a strong sense of community life defined, in part, by rituals peculiar to camp.

SEATED IN THE CENTER of the group is Elbert K. Fretwell, a professor at Columbia Teachers College in New York City. At the time the picture was taken he taught a camp leadership course at the college, which, after John Dewey joined the faculty of Columbia University in 1906, had become the nation's leading institution in developing an educational philosophy based on Progressive social theory. The Progressives felt a need to curb the excesses and problems caused by industrialization and rapid economic expansion. Crime in the cities was on the increase and Americans were becoming too materialistic. The disadvantaged were being left behind. Progressive educators believed they could reform society by

starting with its children, and they came armed with a belief in scientific study, particularly as embodied in the new disciplines of child behavior and educational theory. Progressive camp directors designed camp communities that mirrored the adult communities they wished to create, where campers would learn to live together with respect and justice. They hoped to teach children to solve problems, and strove to teach by example and practice rather than by demonstration and memorization.[22]

Many Progressive educators tried to reform American education from within the public school system, but others started private schools where they could have more control. Like a private school, a residential camp—an isolated community where the educators had twenty-four-hour control of the students—was ideal for putting Progressive theory into practice. Many of the people in the Adirondack Museum photo both were camp directors and had connections to the Progressive Education movement, particularly through private schools. The "bookends" of the group, Julian H. Salomon and Fay Welch, had both taught at the Dalton School, a prominent Progressive school in Manhattan founded in 1919 and still in existence. Welch had founded Tanager Lodge in 1925, and Salomon was assistant director at Camp Miramichi for a time. Both camps were on Upper Chateaugay Lake. In the Lake Placid area in 1921, Mr. and Mrs. Donald Slesinger, who had studied with Dewey, founded Camp Treetops. Camp Collier (Raquette Lake) advertised itself in 1920 as "A School of Natural Development, which stood for advanced and progressive ideals in the science of education."[23]

The enthusiasm of the Progressive educators is largely

ELEANOR DEMING, 1930

Having been active in summer camp work since 1911, I am impressed more each year with the real educational value of the right kind of summer camp. Even the progressive school lacks many of the opportunities for character development and the building up of skills, interests, and hobbies which will fill the leisure time now and through the years. The camp which fails here has missed the way.[58]

EUGENE F. MOSES, 1940

John Dewey, the famous educator, states that the fundamental purpose of Elementary School Education today is not the acquisition of knowledge, but the organizing of habits, impulses, instincts and the general tools of learning. Camp, itself, contributes much to the fulfillment of the cardinal principles of school work but more than that it gives us boys whose habits, ideals, and character are fixed in the formative period by association with unusual leaders.[59]

Carrie Sinn was known to the girls at Camp Severance as "Aunt Bunny." She was photographed at camp in 1929. The Adirondack Museum, P52133.

Julian Salomon (center) teaching Indian lore at a camp leadership course field study at Bear Mountain State Park in the mid-1920s. Courtesy of the Archives of Julian Harris Salomon (private).

responsible for the rapid growth of organized camping in the Adirondacks before the Second World War. Between 1910 and 1920 fifty-four camps were established, and in the decade before the stock market crash, another seventy. Some were short-lived experiments, but a surprising number existed for many years, although not all outlived their founders. Columbia-trained Progressive educators continued to influence the Adirondack camping movement, sending directors and counselors to the region well into the 1940s.

One of the characteristics of Progressivism is professionalization, and training schools, university affiliations, and professional associations are common to most Progressive-era institutions.[24] Organized camping is no excep-

tion. The camp leadership courses run by respected universities (Columbia and Western Reserve) gave the movement academic respectability. The camp directors' associations that grew up before the Second World War organized camp leaders for exchange of information, for publicity, and to establish policies and standards. The first conference of camp leaders was in 1903; in 1910 camp leaders formed the Camp Directors Association, and by 1935 it had become the national American Camping Association.[25]

The profession achieved both a training program and a university affiliation when Columbia University professor Elbert Fretwell established the first collegiate camp leadership course in 1920. The course included a week-long practicum in camping that was sponsored by "various organizations interested in camping,"[26] including the Boy Scouts of America, the YMCA, YWCA, YMHA, the Woodcraft League, and the New York State College of Forestry at Syracuse. The College of Forestry established a Department of Forest Recreation in 1919 that offered various courses of use to camp leaders; in 1930 Fay Welch became Special Lecturer in Organized Camping. Under his direction the college offered courses in nature lore methods, camping techniques, camp administration, and camp leadership. Graduates of Teachers College and the College of Forestry would influence Adirondack camping for years.

In Carrie Sinn's photo, Columbia professor Elbert Fretwell wears a breastplate that looks somewhat like those made of long bone beads worn by Plains Indian men. The breastplate and the presence of Julian Salomon suggest the

Julian Salomon (center) with educators at Bear Mountain State Park, mid-1920s.

other main foundation of the organized camping movement: American Indian culture.

Julian Harris Salomon was at the camp leadership course to teach Indian arts and lore. Salomon was white, but he had studied Indian culture since boyhood trips to the American Museum of Natural History. As an adult, he traveled among the Blackfoot and Pueblo peoples of the American West as well as the Indians of the Mexican Highlands. Salomon was also known as "Soaring Eagle" and "Apota" (Firemaker), the latter name given him by a group of Blackfoot to whom he had taught the use of a bow drill.

Like many other children of the early twentieth century, Salomon had become interested in American Indian culture through the works of Ernest Thompson Seton.

Ernest Thompson Seton in the council ring at Windygoul, 1925.
Courtesy of the Archives of Julian Harris Salomon (private).

Seton, a Canadian, had made enough money as a nature illustrator and author of animal stories by the turn of the century to purchase an estate near Cos Cob, Connecticut, which he named Wyndygoul. In 1901 he caught a group of city boys vandalizing the property. Instead of prosecuting the vandals, Seton invited them to return to the estate the next weekend to camp in his woods. When they arrived, he encouraged them to swim in his lake, climb his trees, and romp to their heart's content. Then, in the evening, he built an Indian-style council fire and regaled the boys with tales of the continent's original inhabitants.

Like many camp directors and educators of the early twentieth century, Seton was concerned about the character and vigor of the American boy. Seton felt his vandals had gone wrong because they hadn't had the right role models and the right environment. The Progressives would have agreed with Seton that the out-of-doors was the right environment for them; where Seton pioneered was in suggesting the American Indian as a model for good character.[27]

Over the next few years Seton developed his theory that given guidance, an appropriate role model, and lots of outdoor activity, the natural instincts of boys could be channeled in a direction that would produce model citizens of upright character. The Woodcraft Indians were introduced to the public in *Two Little Savages,* published in 1903. The story of a contemporary white boy who learns to live like an Indian in the woods near his home one summer, the book was called "a mine of Indian information" by Salomon.[28] *The Birch-Bark Roll,* which Seton first published in 1902, contained even more lore, and gave the blueprint

---

ERNEST THOMPSON SETON, 1927

The Woodcraft League . . . is something to do, something to think about, something to enjoy, something to remember, in the woods, realizing all the time that manhood, not scholarship, is the aim of all true education. It works with a continual recognition of the four ways along which one should develop—the body way, the mind way, the spirit way and the service way. It is, first, last and all the time, recreation—recreation for old and young, male and female. It stresses outdoor life.[S10]

Photograph by Richard Walker.

for Seton's Woodcraft Movement. As Woodcraft Indians, boys were organized into small tribes they governed themselves; adults had only a supervisory role. Honors ("coups") were awarded for achievements and represented by feathers. Boys competed against absolute standards for the coups, not against each other. Indian handicrafts were an important part of the program, as was nature observation and study.

With the arrogance characteristic of many European-Americans of the time, Seton chose only what he felt were "the best examples of the red race" for his Woodcraft Indians.[29] From the Pacific coast cultures he took totem poles, from the Iroquois he took tribal government, from the Plains peoples he appropriated the Omaha Tribal Prayer and the concept of coups. The universal campfire he developed into the Council Fire.

With characteristic Progressive attention to scientific study, Seton consulted experts on Indian culture as he developed his Woodcraft Movement. In 1901 he helped organize the Sequoya League, which was established to work for Indian rights.[30] Another of the Sequoya League's

ERNEST THOMPSON SETON, 1912

Nine leading principles are kept in view [in the Woodcraft Movement]:

1. This movement is essentially for recreation.

2. Camp Life. *Camping is the simple life reduced to actual practice, as well as the culmination of the outdoor life. . . .*

3. Self-government with adult guidance. *Control from without is a poor thing when you can get control from within. . . .*

4. The Magic of the Campfire. *What is a camp without a campfire?—no camp at all, but a chilly place in a landscape. . . .*

5. Woodcraft pursuits. *Realizing that* manhood, not scholarship, *is the first aim of education, we have sought out those pursuits which develop the finest character, the finest physique, and which may be followed out of doors, which, in a word,* make for manhood. . . .

6. Honors by Standards. *The competitive principle is responsible for much that is evil. . . . We try* not to down the others, *but to raise ourselves. . . .*

7. Personal Decoration for Personal Achievement

8. A Heroic Ideal . . . *that is physical, but also clean, manly, heroic, already familiar, and leading with certainty to higher things.*

9. Picturesqueness in Everything . . . *The effect of the picturesque is magical, and all the more subtle and irresistible because it is not on the face of it reasonable.*[S11]

founders, Charles Alexander Eastman, became a lifelong friend and adviser. Ohiyesa, as he was known among his people, was a Santee Dakota Sioux who had taken his medical degree from Boston College and wrote extensively on Indian culture (specifically Sioux) as a model for good character.[31] Seton also consulted scientists such as the ethnomusicologist Alice Fletcher, the Iroquois ethnologist Lewis Henry Morgan, and F. W. Hodge, who wrote the *Handbook of American Indians North of Mexico* for the Smithsonian Institution.[32]

The Woodcraft movement spread rapidly, thanks in no small part to Seton's professional reputation, his flamboy-

Photograph by Richard Walker.

Ernest Thompson Seton dressed as his Indian persona "Black Wolf" at the initial Boy Scout leader training session at Silver Bay in August 1910. Courtesy of the Silver Bay Association.

ance, and his voluminous and popular nature writings. By 1903 there were sixty tribes of Woodcraft Indians scattered across the nation.[33] Seton included girls in Woodcraft at least as early as 1905.[34] The movement also attracted adults. The Camp Fire Club, a conservation organization that Seton had helped found in 1897, met at Wyndygoul in 1904 to observe the Indians.[35] The naturalist John Burroughs visited several times, writing to Theodore Roosevelt in 1906, "Seton has got hold of a big thing with his boys Indian Camp . . . he is teaching woodcraft, natural history and Indian lore in a most fascinating way. I really think it worthy of your encouragement."[36]

In 1906 Seton met the Boer War hero Lt. General Robert S. S. Baden-Powell, who was in the early stages of formulating his own boys' organization in England. Seton gave "B-P" a copy of the constitution and activities of his Woodcraft program, which he had published as *The Birch-Bark Roll,* and B-P promptly used it as the basis for the ini-

---

ERNEST THOMPSON SETON, 1905

[The Woodcraft Indian program] is so plastic that it can be adopted in whole or in part, at once or gradually; its picturesqueness takes immediate hold of the boys, and it lends itself so well to existing ideas that soon or late most camps are forced into its essentials.[S12]

---

tial trial campout of his "boy scouts." Seton intensely resented the appropriation of his scheme without credit and said so publicly, but B-P never acknowledged Seton's contribution to Scouting to Seton's satisfaction. When the YMCA organized the establishment of the Boy Scouts of America in 1910, however, Seton was invited. At the initial Boy Scout encampment at Silver Bay on Lake George, Seton was named Head Scout and led a trial group of boys through a week-long Woodcraft program.[37]

Seton stayed with the Boy Scouts of America until 1915, when he was finally squeezed out of the organization, partly because of his objection to their militaristic tone.[38] He then turned his attention back to the Woodcraft movement, incorporating all tribes into The Woodcraft League in 1917. The league had an impressive roster of advisers that included the northern New York author Irving Bacheller, the publisher Frank Doubleday, Mrs. Thomas A. Edison, and the financier Adolph Lewisohn, whose "Great Camp" Prospect Point would be home to a girl's camp fifty years later.

Unlike the Boy Scouts, the YMCA embraced Woodcraft without altering it. Both organizations valued character development, physical culture, sports, games, and camping. As early as 1905 there were Woodcraft tribes in 235 camps or Y's across the country.[39] It was no doubt gratifying to Seton to see such faithful adoption of his ideas (with acknowledgment), but he had consciously publicized the Woodcraft idea and methods with the hope that all sorts of groups would take them up. Seton's influence on organized camping is much less well known than Woodcraft and the Scouts or the YMCA, but is perhaps his most lasting contribution.[40]

During the second and third decades of the twentieth century, at least eleven Woodcraft camps were founded in the Adirondacks. At Carrie Sinn's Camp Severance, counselor Catherine Kramer was an Eagle Sagamore, "having duly won and publicly been awarded 36 eagle feathers for notable exploits." Camp Miramichi (directors Eleanor and Agathe Deming) and Tanager Lodge followed the Woodcraft program. Cornelia Amster's Camp Che-Na-Wah for Girls, founded near Minerva in 1923, became a Tribe of the Woodcraft League in 1927. Seton sent Amster a "Scroll of Authority" acknowledging that she was "possessed of the true spirit of *Woodcraft*, which aims at the perfect Manhood, whose Joy is in the blue sky, whose Way to Power is self control, and whose Glory is the service of his people."[41]

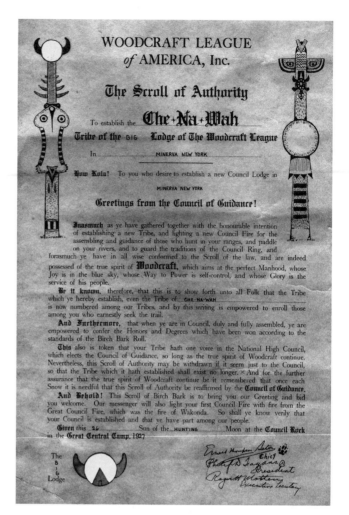

This "scroll of authority" established Camp Che-Na-Wah near Minerva as a tribe in the Woodcraft League in 1927. Courtesy of Ruth and Melvin Wortman, Camps Che-Na-Wah and Baco.

Ernest Thompson Seton at the Merrill House dock on Upper Chateaugay Lake, mid-1920s. The girls were campers at Camp Miramichi. Courtesy of Thomas Campbell.

As Seton predicted, Woodcraft was incorporated into existing camp programs as well. In 1913 Seton himself lit the first council fire at Camp Dudley, which was already twenty-eight years old. Council fires became the most common and best-loved legacy of the Woodcraft movement, but Seton's influence also lived on in awards for feats measured against absolute standards, nature study, and the use of American Indian culture.

The forward-looking Progressive educators and the backward-looking Woodcraft Indians may seem to be odd bedfellows in the development of organized camping, but they did share a faith in scientific study and a debt to the pioneering child psychologist G. Stanley Hall. Hall influenced a generation of educators with his theory of "recapitulation," which posited that children develop just as human civilization had developed, starting in "savagery"

TANAGER LODGE, 1955

The term "wilderness" camping has come up in recent years to distinguish this more rugged form of camping from life in some of the luxurious, country-club type camps. Its sponsors feel that wilderness camping is one of the most valuable and satisfying of all outdoor experiences.

Wilderness camping, [Fay] Welch [founding director of Tanager Lodge] is sure, makes for strength and stability in later life, even if the individual is never actually faced with survival in the wilds.[513]

and moving on to more refined stages of human interaction. Hall's great contribution was to suggest that educators work with this "savage" state, accepting it and playing to it before guiding children, at the appropriate age, to the next stage of development.[42]

A contrast between the up-to-date on the one hand and the traditional or rustic on the other, came to charac-

terize nearly every aspect of camp life by the 1920s as camp leaders shaped a twentieth-century institution in a region as old as the hills. Everyone had an opinion on just how "campy" camp should be. Proponents of what they called "wilderness camping" felt that the environment was the program and camping should aim to teach children to live in and appreciate the outdoors. Others, proponents of what the wilderness advocates called "resort" camps, used the Adirondack outdoors primarily as a setting for their educational endeavors.[43]

By the 1920s children's camps flourished across the Northeast and the upper Midwest. Compared to organized camps in other regions, particularly those close to major cities, Adirondack camps were relatively expensive. By 1925 there was a range of costs for a summer at an Adirondack private camp, but it was still a fairly high range. Few of these camps charged less than $300 for the eight-week season, which would be $37.50 if figured weekly. Most were in the $325—$350 range, and one, Camp Miramichi, charged $400.

Camps run by organizations like the Y's and the Scouts

Boy Scouts in the dining pavilion at Camp Russell, 1918. Courtesy of Alan Woodruff, Camp Russell.

"Hymn to Sainte Jeanne D'Arc." Courtesy of Camp Jeanne D'Arc.

were significantly less expensive. They kept the cost down primarily by offering shorter sessions, generally one or two weeks, and by attracting campers from nearby. Camp Iroquois on Lake George, run by the religious group Gospel Volunteers of the World, cost $7—10 per week in 1910. A week at Boy Scout Camp Russell (White Lake) cost $5.50 for the first week and $5.00 for each additional week in 1918. Transportation costs were high, though, and most organizational camps were patronized by nearby children. Camp Russell, founded in 1918, was the first Boy Scout

Camp in the Adirondacks; it served Scouts from Utica and Rome, less than fifty miles away. By the time of the Second World War there were five Girl Scout camps and ten Boy Scout camps in the region, almost all of them serving upstate councils. Scout camping was enormously popular all over the country and the Scouts were responsible for making a camping experience—however brief—available to more children than private camps or any other not-for-profit organization.[44]

The Y's and other religion-based organizations did bring thousands of middle-class children to the Adirondacks in the years before the Second World War. The Catholic Church eventually founded eleven children's camps in the region. A YMCA worker founded Deerfoot Lodge near Speculator, and Camp Tapawingo, in the same neighborhood, was a spin-off of Camp of the Woods. Costs were kept down with shorter sessions than at private camps, and the programs were less elaborate. Camp Agaming, for example, was sponsored by the Gloversville YMCA, and was also located in the Speculator area. The campers were mostly from Gloversville and nearby Johnstown and Palatine Bridge in the 1930s. Boys camped for most of the summer, but two weeks in August were reserved for girls. Swimming and canoeing were the main activities.[45]

Although children from middle-class families could attend camp in the Adirondacks through the Scouts, the

Campers in front of tent interior, Camp Agaming, 1931. The Adirondack Museum.

EUGENE F. MOSES, 1935

It would be most constructive work to take a group of boys from [the] congregation to an ideal site in the mountains, and there implant in them the seeds which [would] blossom forth in sane, healthful and upright living.[S14]

Photograph by Richard Walker.

Y's, or religious organizations, very few poor children went to camp in the Adirondacks. In contrast, charitable organizations were sending thousands of children to camps closer to the cities by the second decade of the twentieth century. One of the earliest, the Fresh Air Fund (started in 1888), sent poor children to board in country homes, but it also used group camps, including one in Harriman State Park, located on the Hudson just north of New York City. In 1913, the Park Commission began building children's camp complexes and leasing them to youth and social welfare organizations, such as the Boy Scouts and the Association for the Improvement of the Conditions of the Poor.[46] Ruby Joliffe, who appears in the Adirondack Museum camp leadership course photo (page 22), was manager of the children's camps in Harriman State Park.

The African American girl in this picture attended Camp Severance about 1930. She was one of the few children of color who attended camp in the Adirondacks before the 1960s. The Adirondack Museum, P52133.

The vast majority of Adirondack campers before the Second World War were white and not poor. Most were Christians, but Jewish families sent their children to camp in numbers out of proportion to their percentage of the general population. Jews were attracted to camping for the same reasons Christians were—for education and character-building in the outdoors. In the Adirondacks, they established separate camps primarily because Jewish children were not welcome at most camps established by Gentiles until after the Second World War. They had other motivations as well, primarily a particularly high value on education. Sending a child to an Adirondack camp, which was an expensive proposition, also meant that the family had achieved a certain status in American society. The Rabbi Isaac Moses founded the first Jewish camp in the Adirondacks, the Schroon Lake Camp, in 1906, only four years after the foundation of the earliest Jewish camp in the country. The first campers came primarily from uptown Manhattan, a neighborhood with many well-off German Jews. Most attended Moses's Reform temple.[47]

Perhaps Isaac Moses selected Schroon Lake for his

Schroon Lake campers set off for a trip, ca. 1920. Courtesy of the Schroon-North Hudson Historical Society.

FRENCH VACATION CLASS FOR GIRLS, 1896

Many parents have expressed their desire to provide a healthy and pleasant summer outing for their girls as well as for their boys, avoiding for them the evils of life in great hotels, and securing a certain continuity of mental training during the long vacation.[S15]

camp because the community there was prepared to be tolerant of Jews or perhaps the community grew to be tolerant because of his camp and the income it brought to the region. In any case, by the 1930s there were twenty camps on or near Schroon Lake, most of them Jewish, and the "town and gown" seem to have lived in harmony. Entrepreneurs established Jewish resorts and clubs, some of which served kosher food, to serve visiting parents. Jewish camp organizers and campers did not find all other Adirondack communities so tolerant. Libby Raynes Adelman, a camper at Camp Greylock on Raquette Lake in the late 1920s, remembered the residents of the nearby North Point Resort, a Gentile establishment, shouting racial slurs at them as they paddled by the Greylock dock.[48]

MOST OF THE EARLY children's camps were for boys. A notable exception was the French Vacation Class, which existed briefly on Lake Placid only a few years after Sumner Dudley made his first visit to the Adirondacks. It was probably the first exclusively girl's camp in the country.[49] The director, Mlle. Debray-Longchamp, promised "suitable chaperonage" for the "great deal of out-door exercise, both walking and rowing,"[50] that was part of her program. Campers studied French, botany, and sketching, and could get help preparing for college in addition to the outdoor exercise.[51] The program looked very much like that of Pok-O-Moonshine without the sports and with more emphasis on the arts.

Mlle. Debray-Longchamp's venture was short-lived, but it was followed by others. More than one-third of the Adirondack camps founded before the stock market crash were for girls only. Camp Cedar (near Pottersville) and Camp Wabanaki (Lake George), "the most progressive exponent of the camp idea,"[52] were among the many that probably did not last long. Silver Lake Camp, however, en-

This young camper is identified only as "Sarah" in the scrapbook kept by her friend Libby Adelman at Camp Greylock in 1928. Courtesy of Libby R. Adelman.

Photographer Seneca Ray Stoddard labeled this image "Blue Mountain Tramps" when he published it in the 1890s. The women were guests at a local hotel. The Adirondack Museum, P1309.

The campers at the Raquette Lake Girls Club participated in a variety of sports in 1925. Courtesy of Ed and Kathi Lapidus, Raquette Lake Camps.

Lula Mulenberg played basketball at Camp Greylock in the 1920s. Courtesy of Libby R. Adelman.

dured for sixty-one years. Founder Nina Hart, a Brooklyn teacher, planned a camp where girls "might leave city cares and rush behind, sleep and eat in the open, absorb the sun and calm of lake and mountains, learn to stand on their own feet, taking back skills to delight their leisure time and the power of adjustment with companions and friends."[53] The program included riding, tennis, swimming, boating, hiking, baseball, and field sports. In the late 1920s campers from the Theodore Roosevelt Camp for Boys on Lake Champlain camped on Silver Lake and the girls held a dinner and dance for them. Miss Hart reported that the girls then decided " 'no more men!' There were boys enough in winter. Camp was no place for dressing up. It was more fun to wear bloomers and relax."[54]

The growth of girls' organizations paralleled the growth of camping for girls, and in fact the first successful girls' organization started at a camp. In 1888, a couple of years after Sumner Dudley took his first group of boys camping near Kinderhook, Luther and Charlotte Gulick

began taking their daughter and some of her friends as paying customers to their Maine summer home for a few months. The Gulicks named their Maine girls' camp "Wo-He-Lo," a vaguely Indian-sounding acronym that stood for "Work, Health, Love"—their ideals for the American girl. The program of the Gulicks' girls' camp, and of the Camp Fire Girls organization that followed it (1910), were built on the Woodcraft model of Ernest Thompson Seton, with whom they were friends.[55]

Luther Gulick, co-inventor of basketball, co-founder of the Boy Scouts of America, the son of Hawaiian missionaries, and a nationally recognized figure in physical education, did not propose a radical change in woman's role.[56] He and his wife did share with boys' camp leaders a concern for the vigor of America's children, and they designed their Camp Fire program to strengthen girls for their futures as mothers and keepers of the home. In 1912 Juliette Gordon Low founded the other prominent girls' organization of the time, the Girl Scouts of America. Low's program for girls was no more radical than the Gulicks', but her aim of getting girls out of the home and into their communities and the open air was a necessary step toward freeing them from their "separate sphere."

IN 1917 FRANCES SHERIDAN, a teacher in a Progressive elementary school near New York City, purchased a property on The Narrows between the Upper and Lower Chateaugay Lakes. The children at her Camp Kairoa swam, explored the lake in boats, and hiked through the forests around the camp—activities that had become standard for Adirondack children's camps. Unlike most other camps of the day, however, Miss Sheridan's provided many activities intended to encourage the campers' creativity and individuality. And unlike most other children's camps, Kairoa was coeducational.[57]

Adirondack camp leaders were pioneers in coeducational camping.[58] In addition to Kairoa, the Adirondacks Summer Art School (location unknown) and the Gardner-Doing Camp (near Paul Smith's) were also founded in the second decade of the twentieth century. All three empha-

CAMPING DURING THE GREAT WAR

During the summer of 1918, the boys at the Schroon Lake Camp marched and drilled for an hour every evening. Their military training included Close Order Work, the Manual of Arms, and even a few "sham battles." The community came to view drills and a Review on Sundays. Perhaps the Jewish Schroon Lake boys felt an extra need to prove themselves enthusiastic Americans that summer of international war, although other camps demonstrated their patriotism as well. The staff at Camp Dudley, where almost all the boys were white, Anglo-Saxon Protestants, introduced a mass salute to the flag before the evening meal, and taught useful wartime skills such as military drill and ambulance work.[516] [HEB]

SCHROON LAKE CAMP, 1918

So all the Campers contributed their mite to further the cause of preparedness against the day when they might have to fight. Besides the patriotic side of this drilling, it made every boy learn the lesson of obedience without question, and to think and act simultaneously. The true military spirit was inculcated into all.[517]

sized the arts, a particular interest of the Progressive educators. Progressive theory, which aimed to make the school community more like the outside community, also influenced the trend towards coeducational camping, which continued in the pre–World War II years. Coeducational Camp Treetops, Camp Turk (1924, near Woodgate), and Tanager Lodge are still in operation. Of the 213 Adirondack camps founded before 1941, fifteen admitted both boys and girls.

The Outdoor Laboratory

By the time of the stock market crash Adirondack camping had acquired the basic form it would keep for at least the next three-quarters of a century. Some camps evolved along the lines of a boarding school. In these "educational resorts" children lived together for the summer, often in cabins or lodges, and spent most of their time studying or developing skills, many of which, like tennis or baseball, would be useful back in "civilization." Other camps, called "wilderness camps" by a commentator in 1955, remained closer to "camping out." In these camps, children lived in tents or "shacks" and concentrated on outdoor living skills and the study of nature—things done best away from the cities.[59] Despite differences in emphasis, however, most of these camps—whether "resort" or "wilderness," whether private or organizational—were characterized by nature study, campcraft, wilderness travel, water skills, manual training, sports, ritual, and a strong sense of community.

The "camp family" included not only the administrative head (the director) and the campers, but a corps of counselors who were in direct contact with the campers. The larger, more expensive camps might have counselors

ADIRONDACK WOODCRAFT CAMPS, 1928

A well conducted summer camp is practically a necessity for all those who can in any way avail themselves of its unnumbered advantages. It is not a place conducted with the sole purpose of amusing boys for eight or more long weeks during the summer vacation from school, but rather an outdoor laboratory where character and physical fitness are studied and strengthened. . . . We feel that character and those finer things of life which are held in such esteem generally by society cannot by any means be taught, but must be caught.[S18]

whose only responsibility was to teach a skill, but at many camps counselors both taught skills and lived with a small group of children, acting as parent. Somewhat more removed from the campers were the service staff—the cooks, kitchen staff, handymen, and perhaps laundry workers.

Tree identification was a part of nature study at Camp Riverdale in 1930. The Adirondack Museum Library.

By the 1920s, nature study had been an accepted part of formal education and leisure time for over a generation. Hobbyists and schoolchildren alike pondered their relationship to the natural world through scientific observation and aesthetic appreciation. Rock and fern collections, landscape painting, wildlife photography, animal stories such as Ernest Thompson Seton's *Wild Animals I Have Known* (1898), and political action like joining the Camp Fire Association were all legacies of the nature study movement.[60]

Camp nature programs were natural outgrowths of the nature study movement and Seton's Woodcraft movement. "Nature Study is the intellectual side of sport," he wrote in 1912, and identification of plants and animals formed the foundation of many camp nature programs.[61] Seton's *Book of Woodcraft* devotes 160 pages to tree and fungus identification alone. Campers mounted leaves and captured frogs for little natural history museums, or earned awards for learning the natural inhabitants of the woods. "Scout reports," in which children shared their nature observations with others, formed a part of the routine at camps and in Woodcraft tribes.

Camp staff gave each camp's nature program its own character. Some nature programs combined easily with other activities. Seton stressed nature study because American Indians depended on an understanding of their environment; he would have approved of the program at the brother and sister camps Red Wing and Red Cloud on Lake Champlain. In the 1930s the "Wildcraft" program there consisted of four units: nature lore, campcraft, Indian lore, and archery. The campcraft area at the end of the nature trail contained a wigwam and a tipi for campouts and for educating the campers about different native cultures.[62]

Several camp leaders studied forestry in the 1920s, and they took that branch of nature study to their camps. At Syracuse University, the College of Forestry's Department

CAMP DUDLEY, 1922

At present Camp has a very good Herbarium of 125 trees, 20 odd ferns and 125 flowers and mosses. Camp is also fortunate in having a fine collection of insects, moths and butterflies.[S19]

Identification of plants, rocks, and animals was a standard element of nature study at many camps. Some, like Silver Lake Camp in 1957, had special nature study areas for specimens. The Adirondack Museum.

Echo campers prepare their bedrolls for an overnight trip, 1953. Courtesy of Carol Mitchell.

of Forest Recreation offered nature lore and camp management classes. Fay Welch, a graduate of the college, directed the Boy Scout Camp Syracuse on Seventh Lake, where the major activities were trail clearing and improvement. During the summer of 1924 Syracuse campers got practical experience when they helped fight a forest fire on top of Black Bear Mountain. William Abbott, who was on the faculty at the College of Forestry, founded the Adirondack Woodcraft Camp near Old Forge in the same year Welch founded Tanager Lodge. Abbott's campers could take an elementary course in forestry in which they learned surveying, map-making, silviculture, timber cruising, forest protection, and lumbering through field trips and work in their own nursery.[63]

"I've never been lost," Fay Welch declared, "but I've been badly bewildered for three days." That remark is not original, but it summarizes the attitude Welch hoped to instill in a new generation of Adirondack woods travelers.[64]

ADIRONDACK WOODCRAFT CAMPS, 1928

It is on these trips that self-reliance unconsciously becomes a part of each boy's make-up. He learns to care for himself in the woods.[S20]

"Campcraft" as Welch taught it included how to read a map and a compass, start a fire, choose a site and set up an overnight camp, and cook meals.

Fay Welch's father had been an Adirondack guide, a settler who had learned his campcraft by living it. Fay did some guiding in his youth, but then went on to college. He was one of the next generation of camp leaders who came to campcraft later in life. Another was Dillon Wallace, who was a campcraft instructor or consultant to both Pok-O-Moonshine and Dudley in the 1920s.[65] In 1903 Wallace had been part of a small expedition to the unmapped interior of Labrador. Wallace's partner, Leonidas Hubbard, had died there, but Wallace subsequently had a long career traveling and writing about his outdoor adventures.

The goal of campcraft at most camps was to prepare campers for trips away from camp. At the "wilderness camps," campers worked up to the longer hikes, gaining in conditioning and skills through the season. Campers at the private camps had longer to prepare and generally took the most ambitious trips. In the second decade of the twentieth century the Pok-O-Moonshine hiking season culminated in a Mount Marcy trip, which began at camp. The most able hikers climbed the state's highest peak in four days, taking in Whiteface along the way. On the way out they walked along what is now NYS Route 86 from Jay to Wilmington, and the whole way home was thirty-seven miles along "the sometimes hard, but always dusty roads to camp via Eliza-

Severance campers get a ride to the trailhead, ca. 1926. The Adirondack Museum, P52133.

Photograph by Richard Walker.

bethtown and Reber" (today's Routes 73 and 9).[66] Camp Lincoln had a strong emphasis on hiking and had its own hiking club by the time of the Second World War.[67]

Even at the "non-wilderness camps," campers took day hikes and shorter trips, often as an opportunity for nature study. A frequent hike for the Greylock girls was down the North Point Road toward the village of Long Lake—at that time an unpaved dead-end with little traffic. Short hikes did not usually test survival skills, but they did get city children closer to nature than they could be at home, and they gave them a small taste of traveling through the wilderness.

THERE ARE 2,300 LAKES AND PONDS, 1,200 miles of river, and 30,000 miles of brooks and streams draining the Adirondack Mountains. Water, whether a lake, stream, or

river, is the most distinctive feature of most Adirondack camps. Some camps, like the Adirondack Woodcraft Camps and Moss Lake Camp, had private lakes. A few, like Totem Camp, were on rivers (the Oswegatchie) or, like Tapawingo and Camp Eagle Island (Upper Saranac Lake), existed in splendid isolation on an island. Even those that tried to make it without their own waterfront, like Summerhill (near Warrensburg), had an artificial pool for swimming and took campers to a nearby lake for sailing.

Waterfront activities were common to all Adirondack camps. Swimming and paddling a canoe were the basics, rowing and sailing were common, and resourceful waterfront directors (or ones with plenty of resources) taught water polo or aquaplaning. In their "free swim" time, campers could slide down slides into the water, leap off of diving towers, or swoop over the lake at the end of a rope tied to an overhanging branch.

Teaching the campers to swim was the first concern of

CAMP DUDLEY, 1905

A "Shoot-the-chute" was a sensational addition to the deep water swimming equipment last year. It is inclined to the water at an angle of 30 degrees, is 25 feet long, lined with oil cloth, and shoots one into the water at a velocity of something short of a mile a minute.[S21]

At Camp Eagle Cove in the 1950s, as at many other camps, swimmers had to register at the "buddy board" when going in and coming out of the water. Each swimmer had a buddy; the buddies were supposed to stay together and at a signal from the lifeguard they were to clasp and raise hands to be counted. Courtesy of Joan Jacobs Brumberg.

the waterfront director. Through the 1920s the YMCA, the American Red Cross, and the Boy Scouts each had their own swimming instruction programs. In 1931, however, the Camp Directors Association voted to use the Red Cross standards as the official milestones for instruction in swim-ming, lifesaving, diving, boating, canoeing, and camp wa-terfront leadership, as well as in first aid.[68]

Many camps had their own standards in addition to nationally recognized awards. At Camp Greylock, girls worked their way from the green swim cap group through

Swimming lesson at Camp Cedar Isles, ca. 1940. The Adirondack Museum, P44745.

The Camp Che-Na-Wah swimming instructors wore their Red Cross patches on their swimming suits. Courtesy of Ruth and Melvin Wortman, Camps Che-Na-Wah and Baco.

the blues to the white swim cap, at which point they were competent to swim out to Beecher Island, about five hundred yards from the camp dock.[69] Requirements for the Triple Swimmer at the Adirondack Woodcraft Camps were swimming a six-hundred-yard triangle and a three-quarter-mile diamond in Lake Kan-Ac-To, and swimming across the lake fully dressed.[70]

Swimming was not only an important life skill, it was an integral part of the campiness of camp—of what made life at an Adirondack camp so magical and so very different from life at home. It was an important part of the freedom of life in the woods, particularly in the early period before artificial swimming pools were common in cities. Parents were terrified about the health risks of city swimming as well. Polio, or infantile paralysis, seemed to strike disproportionately among children who swam at public pools in the summer. In a pristine lake at camp, parents felt, their children could swim safely.

Once campers could swim competently, they could go boating. The camp fleets of the pre–World War II era reflected the rich variety of small craft available then. When it opened in 1904, the Adirondack Camp on Lake George

provided St. Lawrence skiffs for its boys, "well known as an especially safe boat, and at the same time . . . light and easily rowed."[71] Boats and boating were integral parts of almost every camp program, and in the first half of the twentieth century campers went out in a variety of small craft, from flat-bottomed rowboats to canoes and sailboats. The size of some of the camp fleets was considerable. The best-equipped camps could put all the campers on the water at once. Camp Pok-O-Moonshine boasted enough boats to allow one to every two or three boys—a total of forty small craft at this one camp.[72]

The indigenous boat, the Adirondack guideboat, was not suited to camp use—too expensive, thin-skinned, and tippy for a group of kids. But other types of rowboats were common. Many camps, such as Camp Navarac (Upper Saranac Lake), taught the youngest campers boating safety in flat-bottomed rowboats that were probably built locally. In the second decade of the twentieth century, the rowboats at Pok-O-Moonshine were built by "Old Man Leach," one of two resident carpenters at the camp in the 'teens.[73] Other boats were purchased from factories because good rail access made shipment possible to camps throughout the re-

Lois Shaver (white suit), a physical education major at The Massachusetts Institute of Technology, taught lifesaving at Camp Greylock in 1951. The Adirondack Museum, P68016.

Photograph by Richard Walker.

gion. Boy Scout camps had fleets of Merrimack Skiffs built in Massachusetts by Lowell's Boat Shop.

Sailing was a good activity for teaching self-reliance, and was also regarded as an important social skill by some parents. George H. Longstaff made his new Camp Cedar

Divers ready to take the plunge at Camp Cedar Isles, ca. 1940. The Adirondack Museum, P44501.

The "morning dip," often in the nude, was a good way to wake up and was part of the routine at some single-sex camps, particularly boys' camps. This is Camp Severance for girls, ca. 1930. The Adirondack Museum, P52133.

Camp Navarac had an extensive waterfront program. This 1950s photograph of the fleet shows the rowboats used by the inexperienced campers in the foreground, and in the background Sailfish, a war canoe, tandem canoes, and several larger sailboats. The Adirondack Museum.

Isles (Fourth Lake) a sailing camp when he opened it in the mid-1930s. By 1936 he had inspired an active racing association on the lake in which thirty-six Dunphy Snipes turned out for semi-weekly races.[74]

It was the canoe that really caught on as the quintessential camp boat, however. In the second and third decades of the twentieth century, when children's camping was experiencing its greatest growth, canoes were immensely popular all over the continent for pleasure boating, and camps could buy relatively cheap, stable, durable,

The boys of Camp Windymere on Blue Mountain Lake learned to row as well as paddle in 1918. The Adirondack Museum, P21291.

Sailing at Moss Lake Camp for Girls, ca. 1950. The Adirondack Museum, P43624.

wood-canvas canoes from a number of builders. The Old Town Canoe Company of Maine supplied whole fleets to the region's camps. Canoeing was an advanced skill. Campers had to pass a swimming test before being allowed in a canoe. At camps that also had rowboats, campers had to demonstrate competence in rowing before graduating to canoes.

Canoeing was useful to the camp leader beyond teaching paddling. Campers had to learn to work with at least one other paddler in a canoe—an important skill in itself. Teamwork was nowhere more evident on the water than in the war canoes. Some camps had special camp paddling songs to help keep the crew in cadence. The most common size for a war canoe was twenty-five feet, but the Old Town Canoe Company also built thirty-five-foot war canoes. Crews of six to ten paddled the shorter boats, while the longer ones held twelve to twenty. These extra-long canoes had initially become popular as club canoes in Canada in the late 1890s among groups of men who liked canoe racing but could not afford to own their own boats. Old Town claimed in its 1910 catalog that one of its thirty-five-foot war canoes manned by eighteen young men had beaten every launch it encountered in short sprints on a New Hampshire lake.[75]

Water festivals and "aquacades" gave campers a chance to show off their teamwork and other more esoteric skills. The 1904 Water Carnival at the Adirondack Camp attracted not only parents, many of whom were probably staying at nearby resorts, but members of the vacationing public. They watched rowing and paddling races, diving, swimming, and canoe jousting. Some camp water shows combined skill demonstrations with drama. The Greylock aquacades in the 1950s featured real "floats" with themes from popular shows or literature. At the Silver Lake Camp, girls did synchronized swimming skits as well as water ballet in canoes at their water pageants. The audience sat on shore beyond the dock, which was lined with candle-

RAQUETTE LAKE BOYS CLUB, 1917

But above and beyond all this the red-blooded boy wants the trail, the lake and the stream. He wants to get out into the woods and climb the hills. He wants to launch his canoe on strange lakes and with his kodak penetrate nooks and corners that have perhaps been unexplored since the days of the Indian. And when he is tired and weary he wants to pitch his tent, make his meal over the roaring fire—and then over his coffee swap tales of adventure and sing his songs until over powered by sleep.[S22]

CAMP NAVARAC, 1955

Take a canoe and discover . . .
Discover nature and yourself.
And if you travel far enough on the lake
You'll discover others.

Take a canoe and discover
Continue until life's end
The whole world is open to you
A world of Peace and of Friends.[S23]

Aquaplaning at Echo Camp in the 1950s. Pulling the camper is the 1927 Fay and Bowen launch Echo, *which was purchased for the camp by its original private owners. The boat, and this photo, are in the collections of the Adirondack Museum.*

powered "footlights" made by the camp arts and crafts counselor.[76]

IN 1938 THE CAMP RIVERDALE GLEE CLUB set out from lower Long Lake in three war canoes. They paddled down the Raquette River, hiked over the Indian Carry, and cruised the Saranacs, giving concerts in Tupper Lake, at the Bartlett Carry Club, and at Saranac Inn. (Getting a twenty-five-foot boat around the Raquette Falls carry was not as difficult as it would seem today, because there was a man with a team resident there and he could be summoned by a telephone strung along the carry.) They camped out along the way and again on the way home, and were gone five days. Not many camps combined concerts with canoes, but others sent their campers out on trips of a couple of days or a week or more. Like the hiking trips, canoe trips tested self-reliance and campcraft.

Canoes had a romantic appeal that fit in well with camp mystique and with Seton's ideal of the "picturesque."

Camp Navarac, which had an extensive waterfront program, had a "canoeing campfire" at the end of each season to honor camper achievements in boating. The program included songs, poems, synchronized canoeing routines (team, double, and solo), and the presentation of paddles.

Camp Red Wing on Schroon Lake had a fleet of canoes. The camp launch and a floating slide can be seen in the background of this ca. 1930 postcard. The Adirondack Museum.

War canoe at Camp Eagle Cove, 1950. Courtesy of Joan Jacobs Brumberg.

Boats and paddles formed important parts of camp ritual at other camps as well. At Eagle Cove, campers who had attended camp for five seasons received their own canoe paddle marked with a decal noting their name and dates; Navarac girls received the title of "Captain" when they passed their three-star canoeing test. They then could decorate their own paddle any way they wished, and the paddle remained at camp for future campers to use.[77] Girls who attended Camp Greylock for six years had their names painted on the camp war canoe.[78]

Tanager Lodge, ca. 1925. The camp totem on the bow of the canoe was designed by Ernest Thompson Seton. Courtesy of Tanager Lodge.

Actual "floats" in a parade at Moss Lake in the 1930s. The Adirondack Museum, P43822.

One of the most picturesque boat-related rituals at a number of Adirondack camps was the "wishing boat" ceremony. At Echo Camp (Raquette Lake) in the 1950s, the final campfire of the season concluded with each girl lighting her candle at the central fire and then walking quietly down to the shore of Raquette Lake. There she made her wish for the coming year and set afloat the boat, usually a simple slice of roundwood with a hole in the center for the candle. Camp management hoped for a calm night; watching the flames flickering on the still, dark waters of the lake

was a memorable experience. Camp folklore held that if a boat disappeared during the night the owner's wish would come true. At Camp Jeanne d'Arc on Upper Chateaugay Lake, which had a similar ceremony, counselors remembered rising early the next morning "to make sure that no boats had drifted back to shore."[79]

LANYARDS MADE OF KNOTTED PLASTIC strand have become such icons of organized camping over the past fifty years that one wonders what campers did on rainy days be-

Canoe trip at Camp Cedar Isles, ca. 1950. The Adirondack Museum, P44501.

The final campfire of the camp season, Echo Camp, ca. 1955. The girls are holding their wishing boats. Courtesy of Carol Mitchell.

fore plastic strand. A "boxy, red and white lanyard . . . a useless worthless thing I wove out of boredom" has even been memorialized by a poet laureate of the United States, Billy Collins.[80] By the end of the poem, Collins's lanyard turns out not to be so worthless after all when he gives it to his mother, and certainly many of the craft projects done at Adirondack camps over the years have had symbolic, if not practical value.

The camp arts and crafts idea has its roots in Progressive education's emphasis on manual training and in the Woodcraft movement. *The Book of Woodcraft* suggested making items from Indian cultures across the country,

CAMP CHE-NA-WAH, 1923

A visitor at Che-Na-Wah any weekday except Saturday would be impressed with the fact that Che-Na-Wah is not wholly a play camp. A wide range of arts and crafts are offered, and she would be a most exceptional camper who would not find something to her liking. Every art and craft is under the direction of a trained expert, and the instruction is such as to appeal to campers.[S24]

from Iroquois-style birchbark containers to Navajo looms. Camp craft programs developed along gender lines until the mid-twentieth century. Girls worked on art projects; boys had woodshops. At Camp Walhalla (Lower Chateaugay Lake) in 1905, girls decorated shelf fungus or made baskets "under the tutelage of an Indian basketmaker."[81] At Riverdale and Dudley, boys made stools and boats. At

Campers knotting "gimp" or "boondoggle" at Moss Lake, 1940s. The craft was an old standby at Adirondack camps. The Adirondack Museum, P43135.

Photograph by Richard Walker.

Camp Chickagami on Upper Chateaugay Lake in the early years of the twentieth century campers built canvas-covered kayaks and a Lightning-class sailboat.

"We admit with pride," wrote "Lorry" Hart, editor of the 1913 *Paradoxian*, the yearbook of Camp Paradox (Paradox Lake), "that our Sunday night entertainments are

The boys at Cedar Lodge could make an Adirondack packbasket as part of their crafts activities in the 1950s. Courtesy of Nancy Feldman.

Workshop at the Schroon Lake Camp, ca. 1920. Courtesy of the Schroon-North Hudson Historical Society.

high class enough to be considered treats by critical and discerning audiences." [82] Perhaps he was biased; he was also one of the principals in the "dramatic sketch" of 27 July. Lorenz Milton Hart, who achieved lasting fame as librettist "Larry" Hart with Richard Rodgers on Broadway, continued to hone his dramatic skills when he took a job as dramatic counselor at the neighboring Brant Lake Camp when it opened in 1917.[83] Brant Lake developed one of the strongest traditions of camp dramatics in the region, but by no means the only one. The Paradox thespians produced "dramatic sketches" of Victor Hugo's hero Jean Valjean, but the shows at most children's camps were less serious. Early Dudleyites blacked their faces, persuaded the kitchen staff

CAMP GREYLOCK, 1959

Dramatics is important not only for the child whose special talents are developed but for every child, with or without talent, who is exposed to the joint effort which comprises "the production of a show." To understand that the chorus girl who misses her cue is as important as the star; to understand the tedious repetition and rehearsals that make "good theatre;" to be exposed to talent itself and to develop an appreciation of it; and to watch a script grow from words to a finished performance—these are lessons that I consider of prime value. These are lessons that are valuable whether a child has one line or a major role.[S25]

The girls at Camp Che-Na-Wah made fancy baskets in the 1920s. Courtesy of Ruth and Melvin Wortman, Camps Che-Na-Wah and Baco.

to join them, and worked up a minstrel show that was so popular with the local community that they began presenting it in nearby Westport in the second decade of the twentieth century.[84]

The performing arts are, of course, as easily taught in the cities as in a rustic camp—perhaps more so—and proponents of "wilderness" camps argued that stage productions had no place at camp. Nevertheless, dramatics became a major part of many camp programs, at least at the long-session private school–type camps where campers were resident long enough to rehearse. As minstrel shows passed out of fashion in the adult world outside, they disappeared from camping, to be replaced with melodrama, Gilbert and Sullivan, Broadway shows, and camp-written productions. The drama counselor was probably responsible for the choice of most shows, but campers weighed in as well. There is something almost eerie in the choice of *Lord of the Flies* for the 1993 "Big Show" at Camp Dudley.

Camp leaders may have had different ideas about the relative importance of many elements of a camp pro-

gram—perfecting campcraft or learning landscape painting, for example—but they all agreed on the importance of teaching children to live together. Inspired by the Progressive belief that if children could learn to live well together, they would live well as adults, camp leaders created a camp culture composed of ritual, awards, song, and shared jokes and stories that fostered a sense of belonging. Campers contributed to this culture themselves, as well, with their own jokes, songs, and stories.

Probably the most enduring and common ritual of Adirondack camps is the campfire program. A fire for warmth and cooking had been part of camping out in the Adirondacks forever, but the form it took in organized camping probably came from the Woodcraft tradition. For Ernest Thompson Seton a campfire was not just a way to keep warm, but the heart of the community. In the Woodcraft scheme, the campfire became the council fire, the site of group announcements, recognition of achievement, and entertainment.

The classic Woodcraft council ring provided concentric circles of benches around the fire in the center. The fire was to be laid log-cabin style, not as a "high pyramid or bonfire" or as "a shapeless pile of sticks."[85] Starting the fire was often the beginning of the ritual. At Camp Lincoln and in some Boy Scout ceremonies, a camper or counselor started the fire with a bow drill. Some leaders got rather more theatrical, or, as Seton would have called it, "picturesque," and started the fire with a flaming arrow. At Camp Caravan (Wheeler Pond) in the 1950s, as one camper remembered, the council fire was started by a mysterious figure who ran into the council ring carrying aloft a flaming torch that the camper suspected was a roll of toilet paper

CAMP RIVERDALE, 1960

If boys can learn to get along with one another, to respect one another's different ways, and to work on common projects despite these differences, they will become men who can share a world of less suspicion, less fear, and more happiness. Helping boys grow into such men is the purpose of Camp Riverdale.[S26]

Completion of the hard-surfaced road from Raquette Lake to Blue Mountain Lake in 1929 dealt a mortal blow to steamboat service on Raquette Lake. This excursion steamer, Kiloquah, was beached near the Raquette Lake Girls' Club that year, the boiler and engine removed, and the structure used as an arts and crafts workshop until it became unsafe. Courtesy of Ed and Kathi Lapidus, Raquette Lake Camps.

Dramatics played a big role in the program at the Brant Lake Camp. This play was produced in 1948. Courtesy of Karen Meltzer, Brant Lake Camp.

*The Council Ring at Camp Che-Na-Wah included the totems of the different camp clans on standards
around the perimeter. Courtesy of Ruth and Melvin Wortman, Camps Che-Na-Wah and Baco.*

soaked with gasoline. Copper screens in the fire itself created colorful effects in the flames.[86]

Seton suggested a totem pole for the council ring.
In 1928 Australian carver F. W. Rosher spent the summer
at Camp Riverdale, carving two magnificent totem poles
for its Woodcraft council ring. They were later moved
to a site next to the main building, where they remained
a part of camp life until the camp closed and they were
sold to private individuals. They document the elaborate
ritual and folklore that grew up around some Adirondack camps. Each of the two clans in the Riverdale tribe,
the Stags and the Eagles, had its own pole with the totemic
animal at the top and a cascade of figures, animal and
human, descending from it. The totem poles reinforced
the character lessons the camp was trying to teach:
brotherhood, the sacredness of truth, appreciation of
nature.

Awards for achievement were central to the Woodcraft
system, as in camping in general. In Seton's scheme, these
awards were presented in the council ring. Woodcraft

awards were called "coups," after the Plains Indian custom
of ritual killing. In many Plains tribes, a warrior "counted
coup" by riding up to an enemy in battle and touching him
with his coup stick. He was then allowed to mark the stick
or some other possession of his to commemorate the coup,
and to tell about it around the council fire. Seton's honors
system was based on absolute standards rather than competition against one's peers. He deplored "the competitive
principle," feeling that it focused attention and resources
on a few champions while leaving out the majority.

Woodcraft coups were originally actual feathers. Some
camps, such as Camp Lincoln, gave feathers, but by the
1920s Woodcraft awards were little embroidered patches
shaped like feathers that were sewn on an over-the-
shoulder felt band. Scouting merit badges, which were
modeled on the Woodcraft coups, were also fabric patches,
but each was different and pictured the activity that was
being recognized.

The merit badge or "coup" idea became a part of camp
life. By the 1940s and 1950s Adirondack camps gave little

Totem pole of the stag clan, Camp Riverdale, 1928. Private collection; photograph by Richard Walker in the Adirondack Museum exhibit.

cloth patches or other awards for everything from identifying ten species of bird or starting a fire with only two matches to making one's bed. When the Greylock girls accomplished the swim to Beecher Island and back, they received a silver pin in the shape of an anchor; Girl Scouts received a patch with a seahorse embroidered on it for a similar feat in Lake Clear. Campers at Navarac, who tended to return for several years, worked to acquire little pictorial patches for effort in dance, athletics, music, diving, campcraft, boating, tennis, canoeing, crafts, sailing, drama, swimming, and waterskiing. As campers achieved certain standards, they were awarded letters, such as an "N" for tennis, "A" for athletics, "V" for swimming, and so on. After earning any four letters they received a pillow; for re-earning four letters after completing "NAVARAC," they were awarded numbers designating the year.[87] What became at some camps like Navarac a complicated system of progress

CAMP RIVERDALE, 1928

The Totem Pole

Hear the saga of the Totem,
Learn the wisdom and the lore
Of the ancient, ageless forests,
Of the suns and moons of yore,
For the forest teaches knowledge,
Bravery and strength of heart.
Tells the stripling and the weakling:
"Be a Man, and play your part." [S27]

reports and awards was in part a result of what one historian has called "the nation's infatuation with scientific management and measurable outputs" in the Progressive era.[88]

By the 1950s, camps had adopted the standards of national organizations in several skills areas. Many camps used the swimming standards of the American Red Cross and the archery standards of the Camp Archery Association. In addition, camps such as Camp Eagle Feather (Raquette Lake) and the Raquette Lake Camps used the standards of the American Water Ski Association. Eagle Feather campers also learned outboard motor operation according to the standards of the New York State Conservation Department, and Deerwood Adirondack Music Cen-

Many camps had totem poles, not all of which were erected in the council ring. These two formed part of a gate at the Adirondack Woodcraft Camp. "Chief" William Abbott rides the horse. Courtesy of John Leach, Adirondack Woodcraft Camps.

MEENAHGA LODGE, 1930–32

The camp chart is a record of individual effort and achievement. Each boy's name is on it, and every evening in Assembly he tells whether or not he has won a star to be put on it that day, in any of the thirty-five headings under the five main divisions of Watersports, Landsports, Wood-craft, Campcraft, and General. There are four sizes of letters to be won through the individual chart work, the hat letters, the sweater letters, the monogram, and the highest honor the chart can offer, the emblem. The nurse holds First Aid classes, the nature counselor conducts Nature Study work, there are daily marks for personal and room neatness, and accomplishments in all these branches are recorded on the chart. The divisions under each heading grade from simple to difficult, and cover all the phases of camp life and work, so that the chart offers possibilities to the youngest and the oldest boy, in every field of interest.[528]

Photograph by Richard Walker.

ter gave New York State Regents credit for some of its music courses.

The ultimate award at many camps was an all-around good character award. Camp Dudley awarded its first "camp emblem" in 1906. It required excellence in athletics and water skills and knowledge of campcraft, nature, and a craft, as well as outstanding social skills and moral qualities.[89] In 1927, after the first season at Adirondack Wood-craft Camps, "Chief" Abbott presented his hunting knife to the boy he considered the outstanding camper of the summer. The "Chief's Knife" tradition has continued, as many such traditions have, becoming part of the camp culture.[90]

The coveted good character awards seem to have been used mostly at the summer-long private camps, where the long session gave time for leaders to get to know the campers. Among the organizational camps, Boy Scout Camp Russell—with its own long traditions and the traditions of the Scouting organization behind it—offered a high honor award for character that was based on an interpretation of Indian ritual and is similar to one with a different symbol that is still part of life at Deerfoot Lodge. One Russell boy called the award "the equivalent of the Congressional Medal of Honor."

Initiation for the Russell award began with a solo overnight trip modeled on the Plains Indian vision quest. The Scouts performed this clad only in a blanket and moccasins, and were cautioned not to speak, eat, or sleep for "one circle of the sun." The Scout leader in charge of the quest appeared in the dark and tormented the camper with food and showed up again during the day impersonating an irate farmer in an attempt to trick the Scout into speaking. If the Scout successfully completed the solo, he returned to camp for an Indian sweat bath and a ceremony with other initiates. The Scout honor was called the Order of the White Swastika. For obvious reasons it was discontinued by the end of the 1930s, although Scouts nationally still strive for a similar good character award, the Order of the Arrow.[91]

The Scouts abandoned the White Swastika symbol because of its appropriation by the German Fascists, but many other interpretations of American Indian culture became firmly entrenched in Adirondack camps. Some held Indian pageants. In the 1930s the pageant at Camp Lincoln featured an attack on pioneers in a covered wagon, who were then brought to the Indian village, followed by an Indian council at which peace was declared.[92] At Red Cloud, as at many camps, campers were taught how to make fires with a bow drill, how to communicate using Indian sign language, and how to perform traditional Indian dances. In 1937 they learned, for example, "the symbolic moose dance," which featured two campers in the role of the moose and "the challenging call of the bull moose on [an Indian] birch horn."[93]

Just as Ernest Thompson Seton had legitimized his Woodcraft Indians by using scholarly research, some camp leaders employed "real Indians" as staff. The basketmaker who taught at Camp Miramichi was likely a maker of fancy baskets from the nearby Mohawk reserve at Akwesasne. Other Indian counselors came certified as authentic by the federal government; in the 1930s the National Youth Administration ran an Indian camp counselor program. In the 1940s and 1950s Indians were actively recruited for

Oren Lyons, a member of the Onondaga Nation, was a counselor at Camp Onondaga on Long Lake in the late 1940s. In this photo he does an Iroquois dance at the weekly Indian Council. Campers received their feathers for achievements of the preceding week at the council in addition to watching Iroquois dances. Courtesy of Alan Jones.

MOSS LAKE CAMP, 1945

Our Honor Girl Creed

An Honor Girl is in every sense a model camper. She enters wholeheartedly into all activities and is conspicuous for her fine spirit and attitude. In everything which she undertakes she is outstanding because of her effort and earnestness. She includes everyone in her circle of friends and is at all times congenial with all with whom she has contact. She is always a good sport, a graceful winner and a cheerful loser. Her personality is one which permeates the entire group and serves as a model, aiding more passive personalities to develop individually. She is not the center of her own world, but rather often disregards her personal wishes in an effort to make others happy. She accepts things as they come without criticism and tries by her own example to encourage optimism and cheerfulness. She is thoughtful and constantly on the alert for ways in which she may be helpful to others. Her attitude toward the counsellor [sic] staff is one of obedience and respect. She is ever willing to do her utmost for her team and her enthusiasm and spirit send forth an enlivening spark that kindles the flame of friendship and good will among her companions.[S29]

work in children's camps. In the Adirondacks, there were Indian counselors at Camp Eagle Cove, Camp Triangle (near Saranac Lake), and Camp Onondaga (Long Lake). Cooper French, the director of Onondaga, hired several young men from the Onondaga Reserve near Syracuse. One of them, Oren Lyons, took a one-week course in camp counseling, probably given by a YMCA near his home, before setting off for his summer job. Lyons was a member of a dance troupe on the reserve, and the Iroquois social dances he performed for the boys at Camp Onondaga were important parts of the weekly campfires.[94]

In the popular mind, American Indian culture fit in well with the Adirondack wilderness. After all, this is the region of Cooper's Uncas, Hawkeye, and Chingachgook. Adirondack camp culture included Indian names. Camp Chingachgook on Lake George and two Hawkeyes (Silver Lake and Lake George) commemorated fictional Indians, as did Camps Meenahga, Nokomis (Rainbow Lake), and Owaissa (Indian Lake) from Longfellow. There were two Camp Algonquins (Lake George and Summit Lake), two Cherokees (Upper Saranac Lake and Lake Champlain), an Iroquois (Lake George), and others like Niqueenum (Lake Champlain), Wah-Na-Gi (Lake George), Hoh-Wah-Tah (Star Lake), and Nawita (Paradox Lake) from real or imag-

A bed-making race was part of the competition of Color War at Camp Eagle Cove in the 1950s. Courtesy of Joan Jacobs Brumberg.

ined sources. Camp staff were given Indian names, like "Chief" William Abbott of the Adirondack Woodcraft Camps, "Chief" Herman Beckman of Camp Dudley, and "Chief" Colba Gucker of Camp Lincoln. Mrs. Gucker, also active in camp life, was called "Mrs. Chief." Even at a music camp (Deerwood on Upper Saranac Lake), the director, Sherwood Kains, was called "Chief."

At many of the camps with summer-long sessions, ritual and competition came together in an all-camp event lasting a week at some camps. Brant Lake Camp claims origination of the event, dating it to 1917.[95] All campers were assigned to a team that competed in a wide variety of events. Points could be earned for skills taught at camp, such as swimming or canoeing, or for less serious accomplishments. At Camp Lincoln the big competition was an "Indian Week"; at many camps it was called "Color War" because each of the camp teams was named for one of the camp colors. The all-camp competition was one of the things that campers remembered and shared, and it was also a needed break in the camp routine.

Color War often started by surprise. At Woodmere and at Navarac the director broadcast Khachaturian's "Sabre Dance" over the camp loudspeaker system in the middle of the night as a notice for all campers to assemble for their team assignments. To be chosen a team captain was a signal honor. Song competitions, dramatic skits, and drills requiring the cooperation of all members of the team were common, as was a long and complicated treasure hunt or

relay race. At Navarac in 1969 one of the relays involved teams of three campers, each of whom had to run through shallow water to an anchored boat, climb in, take a cracker from the counselor waiting there, eat it, then sing "Row, row, row your boat" through once, and run back to shore.[96]

The all-camp competition became something that distinguished camp and that all campers shared, as did the camp religious rituals. Many camps, both Christian and Jewish, had distinctive regular weekly religious services, often at an outdoor "chapel." These outdoor chapels were part of a long tradition of seeing the Adirondack wilderness as a special abode of God. Both Jewish and Christian services tended to be informal.

Most Adirondack Jewish camps were Reform and usually had only one service a week, either on Friday night or Saturday morning. By the 1950s even the more "religious" Jewish camps, such as Che-Na-Wah, which was endorsed by the Conservative Synagogue of America in the 1920s and had started out with two weekly services, celebrated only one. Jewish Camp Severance called its Saturday gathering "Serious Hour." Serious Hour, like many camp religious services, Jewish and Christian, was a time to discuss ethics and morals, with perhaps a sermon by an older camper or counselor. Some camps, like Che-Na-Wah and Camp Swastika (Fourth Lake), also served kosher food. Aside from these distinctions, however, the programs at

Sabbath service at Camp Eagle Cove, ca. 1950. Fourth Lake is in the background. Courtesy of Joan Jacobs Brumberg.

The Counselors in Training took charge of the service in the outdoor chapel at Silver Lake Camp, 1948.
The "chapel" was a series of rock ledges facing the lake, to the left in this photo. The Adirondack Museum.

Adirondack Jewish camps were similar to those at Adirondack camps attended by Gentiles.[97] This is in marked contrast to what was happening elsewhere in the Northeast. By the 1920s, many Jewish camp leaders designed their programs to strengthen the American Jewish community by educating children in Jewish ways of living and thinking.

Religious ritual at camps attended primarily by Christian children was typically some sort of gathering on Sunday morning. Services were generally informal and ecumenical with perhaps hymns or an abbreviated liturgy, but usually consisting primarily of a prayer and an inspirational talk from a counselor or camper. Catholic campers were required by their religion to attend Mass every Sunday in a consecrated church. Nondenominational camps took campers to church in the nearest town; Catholic camps had chapels on-site. The chapel at Jeanne d'Arc was dedicated to the namesake, who founder Ruth Israel felt would be an inspiration to girls. Mass was typically celebrated there by a visiting priest.

The strong sense of community that often developed at camp—especially at the private camps with summer-long sessions—was also created by the campers themselves

as they shared unplanned experiences and planned jokes.[98] Short-sheeting the counselor's bed, midnight raids on the cookie supply, and spontaneous activities all helped create a bond among the campers, something they could share only with other campers.

Camp songs became part of the shared experience that helped define the camp community. Progressive educators liked to use song in the classroom, and most camps, both private and organizational, developed a rich tradition of songs. There were songs for mealtimes, songs for religious services, songs for the mornings and for the end of the day. There were songs written by the staff to remind the campers of good behavior and good posture, and songs commemorating the foibles of counselors written by the campers themselves.

Song formed a bond among campers and identified them in the community. In 1913 the boys from the Schroon Lake Camp went into town for a day of athletic contests against the staff at the Leland House hotel. After the games they marched single file into the Grill Room for dinner, singing their marching song. During the meal, the various tables burst forth with several original cheers, and after the

CAMP DUDLEY, 1923

We had a snipe hunt Tuesday night. I always thought snipe were little birds that went around on the ground on dark nights and you hunted them by getting lights and blinding the snipe and then beating the ground around them and driving them into a bag. Ted Russell who was in charge of the snipe hunt said there were two kinds of snipe. The snipe we were supposed to be hunting were little brown animals about 8 inches long and about 4 inches high and that they bite and have very sharp tails which they use as a formidable weapon of defense. We started off and as we got out to the hunting ground we began to hear little growls. Then one fellow would yell I see one and we would run wildly around trying to find it. And almost everybody would think they saw one but I saw nothing. Sometimes I think I haven't got a good imagination. One fellow was reported having fallen out of a tree and killed himself but I heard him laugh as the fellows carried him back to camp. I think the whole thing was fishy because after the fellow fell out of the tree a "snipe" that looked like a boy climbed out of the tree and ran away on his hind legs. Wednesday night if there's a full moon we will have another snipe hunt.[S30]

Bunk signs were a way for campers to personalize their living space without damaging the walls of the bunk. Photograph by Richard Walker.

meal they headed for camp, again singing their marching song.[99] It must have been a memorable day for the campers—and for the guests at the hotel.

Organizations like the Scouts and church groups came to camp with a ready-made, commonly known repertoire; organizational and private camps alike created their own songs peculiar to camp. Campers were expected to learn camp songs, for Dudleyites the hymns in the *Camp Dudley Hymnal* for example, or the "Omaha Tribal Prayer" for the boys of Idylwold (Schroon Lake). The prayer was included in Seton's *Book of Woodcraft*. In making up their own songs to celebrate, to commemorate, or for Color War competition, campers commonly set new words to a well-known tune. Camp songbooks have lost much of their meaning for readers today because so many of the tunes are lost to us, but one can still imagine a hall filled with three hundred Dudleyites singing "We've Been in the Adirondacks" to the tune of "I've Been Working on the Railroad."

Progressive educators felt that schools and camps that were informal and child-centered would be better learning environments than ones that were regimented and formal. Adirondack camps tried to create a homelike atmosphere by arranging the campers in "families" that slept and ate together with a counselor who took the role of the parent. In an era when children didn't dare call an unrelated adult by

CAMP GREYLOCK, 1965

Greylock Camping Song (Tune: "Aura Lee")

Far from the city's rushing streams,
Far from strife and care,
Lies the haven of our dreams,
Greylock Camp, so fair.
Greylock Camp, there it lies,
Under the skies so blue.
We will ever sing thy praise,
To thee we'll e'er be true.[S31]

Counselor singing group, Camp Whippoorwill, 1964. Courtesy of North Country Camps.

his or her first name, "Mr." or "Mrs." still seemed too formal for camp. Camp adults were often known by familiar, family-like titles such as "Aunt Bunny" of Camp Severance (the Carrie Sinn of the camp leadership photograph), "Aunt Helen" of Totem Camp, "Uncle Sid" of Camp Eagle Cove, or "Mother Cornel" of Camp Che-Na-Wah. Camps also used other types of leaders' names such as "Skipper" Clough at Echo Camp or "the Colonel" (a woman) at Camp Jeanne d'Arc, to make the adults more accessible.

Camp leaders, as surrogate parents, took on all the roles of the real parents while children were in camp. The counselors at Idylwold identified the bed-wetters among the boys and woke them up in the middle of the night for a trip to the bathroom. Counselors inspected hands before meals, cautioned campers to wait until all had been served

CAMP WOODMERE, 1980

Perfect Posture (Tune: "Row, Row, Row Your Boat")

Perfect posture, perfect posture,
Do not slump, do not slump.
Straighten up your backbone
Straighten up your backbone
Watch that hump, watch that hump.[S32]

The boys at the Adirondack Woodcraft Camps had their hands inspected before every meal in the 1950s. Courtesy of John Leach, Adirondack Woodcraft Camps.

Boys writing their required letters home, Schroon Lake Camp, ca. 1940. Courtesy of the Schroon-North Hudson Historical Society.

to begin meals, and made sure the campers brushed their teeth. Camps tried to reinforce the camper's bond with home as well, by urging campers to write to their parents. At Camp Eagle Cove on Fourth Lake, as at many camps, campers had to present a letter home to get into the dining hall; at Eagle Cove, they had to write three times per week.

If counselors took the role of parents to the campers, directors often took the role of parents to the counselors. Counselors at Echo Camp, which was accessible only by water, were allowed to leave camp one or two nights a week on a rotating basis. The camp caretaker would drive them in the camp launch to any one of the five hotels on Raquette Lake and then pick them up at a prescribed hour. When the counselors returned to camp, each was required to visit

---

CAMP CHATEAUGAY

I was so homesick during my brief stay at Camp Chateaugay that I begged my parents to come take me home. A friend of mine was a regular camper and encouraged me to come but I was not ready for independence from my parents! I promised I would give my sister, Florence, all my toys if I was rescued.[S33]

Mail call, Echo Camp, 1953. Courtesy of Carol Mitchell.

"Skipper" in her cabin to say good night and, incidentally, to give the director a chance to see that they hadn't had too much to drink.[100]

Most camp leaders tried to provide homelike supervision for their charges, but they did not all agree about how up-to-date to be in camp living arrangements. On the one hand, camp leaders wanted to satisfy parents that their children had all the facilities that the most up-to-date child-rearing professionals said they should have and, on the other hand, the whole camp idea was based on camping *out* and living close to nature without modern conveniences. This mixture of civilization and wilderness, rustic and modern, has characterized Adirondack camp life throughout its history.[101] The debate over "campiness" was particularly pronounced on the subject of sleeping and eating.

By the 1920s, camp leaders began promoting use of buildings for sleeping rather than tents. Canvas wall tents may be adventurous and romantic, but they take a great

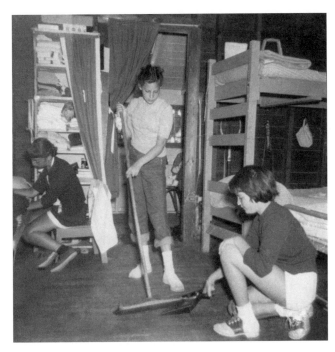

Lynne Littman, Judy Leibowitz, and Marjorie Malina clean their bunk at the Raquette Lake Girls' Camp, 1953. Courtesy of Marion Lazar Usher.

Camp Severance, 1943. The Adirondack Museum, P52133.

deal of maintenance, the interiors get muddy or dusty (depending on the weather), and they can leak and blow down. Scientists in the new field of public health began questioning the wisdom of tents as well, because of the dangers of dampness and crowding. Tents were cheaper than buildings, however, and because of the romance and the cost they are still used even today at some Adirondack camps.[102]

The first "improvement" to tent living was a wooden platform on which the tent was erected, which kept the interior cleaner and dryer. Then in the late 1920s, small cabins, variously called "bungalows," "shacks," or "bunks," appeared on the Adirondack camp landscape. In 1930 "the

ARTHUR T. WILCOX, 1941

The kind of sleeping quarters which a camp utilizes is an extremely important factor in determining its character and value as an interesting and satisfactory outdoor environment. . . . Sleeping in a tent stands as an especially strong symbol of high adventure and romance to the camping youth of today.[S34]

midgets," the youngest campers at Wakonda, slept in bungalows.[103] Dormitories were the least desirable sleeping accommodations, from all perspectives except cost. They were most often found at low-budget camps, of which the Adirondack region had relatively few.[104]

Shacks may have muted the sound of the wind sighing in the trees, but camp planners made sure campers still had plenty of fresh air through large windows. The lodge at Silver Lake Camp had sleeping porches on all four sides. Some bunks were variants on the Adirondack lean-to, a structure with three walls, a roof that sloped toward the back, and a front that was completely open. The lean-to spread out into the wider world of camping; at Girl Scout camps in the Rockies during the 1960s, campers slept in lean-tos that were called, simply, "Adirondacks."

Often the camps concentrated their money for capital improvements on group buildings rather than "bedrooms." First in importance was the dining hall, and next was a building where campers could congregate in bad weather. In the 1920s, Riverdale director Frank Sutliffe Hackett engaged the well-known rustic architect Augustus

"Midget's Bungalows," Camp Wakonda, near Pottersville, 1930. The Adirondack Museum, P13926.

Shepherd to design a library, dining hall, and lodge, all made of local stone, but he had the older boys sleeping in tents into the 1940s.

Adirondack camping has a distinctively regional variation on camp housing. A number of former "Great Camps," complexes originally built as private estates, became children's camps as their owners' fortunes changed. There, campers used the same guest cottages and lodges that had housed New York society a generation before. Sara Blum purchased financier Adolph Lewisohn's Prospect

Rest hour for the Juniors at Silver Lake Camp, 1959. The Adirondack Museum.

Point for Camp Navarac in 1952 and Frances Clough bought Echo Camp, which had been built by the governor of Connecticut, in 1946. Other camps were given "Great Camps" or purchased them at reduced prices. Scout groups were the beneficiaries of several of these deals; the Durant-designed Camp Uncas and Camp Sagamore became Boy Scout camps, and Levi Morton's Camp Eagle Island became a Girl Scout camp.

Girls were often treated somewhat differently from boys when it came to camp housing. When the Dudley boys were sleeping on the ground, the girls of the French Recreation Class were sleeping in buildings that were "convenient and very comfortably furnished," with sanitary drainage.[105] In 1910, well before the Wakonda midgets got their shacks, Silver Lake Camp director Nina Hart engaged a builder to erect a stone lodge for her campers to sleep

CAMP CHE-NA-WAH, 1923

Experience has taught that the bungalow affords the highest degree of comfort and convenience of Camp shelters. It is airy, dry, well lighted, and combines privacy with perfect ventilation. Each bungalow is equipped with a bath room, and accommodates five campers and a counsellor [sic]. Single spring mattress beds are provided.[S35]

Echo Camp girls bunked in the guest cabins and family quarters of the summer home of former Connecti-cut governor Phineas C. Lounsbury, who built the camp in 1883. The camp's founding director, Frances "Skipper" Clough, purchased the camp from the governor's heirs in 1946. The Adirondack Museum.

in.[106] Some of the "school" camps also housed their boys in buildings. In the case of Meenagha Lodge, this was a preexisting camp owned by a faculty member of the Adirondack-Florida School.

In addition to their theories about camp housing, the scientific child-rearing professionals had a great deal to say about children's diet. Since the days when James Hankins served up steak, potatoes, and ice cream to the boys of Pok-O-Moonshine, camps prided themselves on serving plenty of wholesome food. In the 1920s they began to stress hygienic preparation and nutrition. The State of New York had begun inspecting the water supplies at children's camps in 1914; in the 1920s the inspections began to include food service.[107]

The quality of camp food depended on the camp budget. Dishes like "Creamed Mushrooms and Carrots on Split and Buttered Shredded Whole Wheat Biscuits"[108] (from a 1937 Kellogg's camp cookbook) were probably more common than the grilled cheese sandwiches served at Echo Camp. At Echo, camp cook Mary Smedley gave campers their choice of cheddar or Swiss cheese on rye, pumpernickel, or white bread.[109]

Before good transportation routes and refrigerated trucks, fresh food was purchased locally. Matthew Ryan, the guide at Pok-O-Moonshine, sold the camp fresh veg-

CAMP DUDLEY, 1924

I have found out that the ses pool for the toilet is under the Indian pageant grounds. Too bad isn't it. The waste water is emptied into the stream that flows under the pretty little bridge in the gulley on the way over to the outdoor chapel. It smells fierce. Personally considering the cost I would prefer the old "Inciny." We have three names that we call the new flush toilets. The most common is "The Institute. . ." There are ten seats on each side. The water flows in one end every fifteen minutes and out the other end. It doesn't splash.[S36]

"Fort Pergatory" [sic], a lean-to style bunk at Adirondack Woodcraft Camps, 1960. The Adirondack Museum, P15900.

etables and milk from his farm. By the middle of the twentieth century, however, fresh vegetables and milk were coming from local towns and other supplies came in cans and boxes from more distant markets. In the 1950s Camp North Star near Duane bought its meat from a butcher in Malone; lettuce and other vegetables came from a grocer in Saranac Lake. Bread mixes and cereals were ordered from New York City. Today, camp food comes off the same trucks that supply the region's restaurants.

CAMP CHE-NA-WAH, 1923

The kitchen is in charge of an expert chef who is guided by a dietitian. The Camp maintains a "table" liberally supplied with well-cooked, tasty food. The vegetables are from a nearby farm, the milk from a nearby dairy, and the eggs strictly fresh, are collected in the immediate vicinity. No canned goods are used.[S37]

In the years before the late-twentieth-century epidemic of childhood obesity, when a skinny child might be a sickly child, kids were fattened up at camp. "Uncle Sid" and "Uncle Bello" ran a "milk and cookies club" at Camp Eagle Cove in the 1950s. The members were children felt to be too scrawny. The club met before bedtime. Camps could also help children watch their weight. Many prohibited food shipments from home, especially of candy, and they could regulate the camp food as well. Gail Bosch went the entire summer of 1946 without a single dessert at Moss Lake Camp because she was deemed in need of slimming.[110]

Camp Che-Na-Wah claimed that that "no canned goods are used" in its kitchen.[111] Campers on the trail could make no such boast. Canned goods were heavy to carry, but offered a wide variety of meals to the creative camp cooks. Riverdale campers must have left a trail of tin cans from Long Lake to Saranac Lake on their 1938 Glee Club trips. They ate canned fruits for breakfast (prunes, apricots, peaches, or pears in #10s), canned meat sandwiches for

Dining hall at Camp Eagle Cove, 1948. Courtesy of Joan Jacobs Brumberg.

lunch (sardines, corned beef, ham, or salmon), and canned stew or pork and beans for dinner.[112] Although the boys of Camp Riverdale were not overly creative with their meals—making a spaghetti sauce with nothing but tomato paste and cheese, for example—the girls of the Silver Lake Camp made more elaborate meals. In the 1950s a counselor who was a home economics major at Russell Sage College taught them reflector oven cooking as well as main dishes for the frying pan and pot. Many, such as "Ring Tum Diddy"—a "fry pan dish" of onions browned in bacon fat, then warmed with canned tomatoes, cream-style corn, and

cheese—were meant to be served over toast or pasta. Applesauce and graham cracker pie or blueberry upside-down cake must have tasted especially good on the trail, even though the applesauce did come out of a can.[113]

The Progressive educators' interest in making the schools more like the real world extended to the dining rooms of children's camps. At private camps campers ate in small groups and served themselves family style. Some camps had waiters or waitresses, usually older former campers who wanted to spend another summer at camp or current campers on work detail. Larger institutional camps

---

CAMP EAGLE COVE, 1974

To Whom It May Consern,
*   I'm hungry!!! Very hungry and I would like you to send food.*
*   Love, ADAM [S38]*

CAMP GREYLOCK, CA. 1960

Dear Anyone,
*   I am going to have a hungry brache down there is not onof food I am always starved to death*
*   Love, Lori [S39]*

Many camps had small stores or "canteens" where campers could purchase sundries. Candy was often carefully regulated at camp, although campers eagerly awaited shipments from home. At Echo Camp, campers could shop at a wheeled cart with a locking cover that was open at specified times of the day. The Adirondack Museum, P68098.

Camp cookery with a reflector oven, Silver Lake Camp, 1948. The Adirondack Museum.

Mary Smedley making grilled cheese sandwiches for the girls at Echo Camp about 1960. The Adirondack Museum, P68052.

generally needed to serve more children more cheaply and often seated the children at long tables and had them get their own food from a cafeteria line that was more like that found in the military.

Echo Camp's Mary Smedley was an African American woman whose husband was a coal miner in West Virginia. She cooked at Echo Camp for many years, usually bringing sisters or friends with her. Echo was accessible only by water and she and the other kitchen staff rarely left its point of land; she may not have felt any more isolated there than in town. The Adirondack region was overwhelmingly white. The presence of so many black camp cooks—at Pok-O-Moonshine, Cedar Isles, Deerwood, and Minnowbrook (Lake Placid), to mention a few—speaks not only of the limited employment opportunities for African Americans

Staff at Moss Lake Camp, ca. 1945. The Adirondack Museum, P43821.

Fred Ives sliding down the roof slide at the Camp Navarac carnival, 1963. Ives, a Saranac Laker, was the camp caretaker and all-around handyman, doing jobs that ranged from shoveling the roofs in winter to making all the banquet favors for the final dinner of the camp season. The Adirondack Museum.

but of the common camp practice of bringing in most staff from outside the area.

Children's camps were an important part of the seasonal economy in the Adirondacks. Even though most of the staff—directors, counselors, and many cooks—have come from out of the area, local residents have benefited from local purchases at grocery and hardware stores, and local residents have added camps to their list of clients for occasional jobs such as trucking. Until private cars became widely used, several men in the North Creek area supplemented their income by moving campers and their gear

CAMP OF THE WOODS, 1935

The Village of Speculator which I have the honor to represent, regard you and your enterprise as a valuable asset not only from a monetary standpoint but in various ways. . . . In transforming a wilderness of little value, inhabited only by wild life, to the attractive and valuable property of the "Camp of the Woods" as now constituted is an asset to our village which should not be underestimated.[S40]

CAMPING DURING THE GREAT DEPRESSION AND WORLD WAR II

Millions of people across the country were standing in soup lines in the 1930s, but to George H. Longstaff the Great Depression was "a cloud with a silver lining."[S41] Longstaff was an entrepreneur in the Fulton Chain area who had opened the Moss Lake Camp for Girls in 1922. By the 1930s he had built up a good working relationship with Moses Cohen, an Old Forge businessman who held the mortgages on a number of area properties. When Cohen foreclosed on them between 1933 and 1941 Longstaff acquired Camps Cedar Island (which he renamed Cedar Isles), Lo-Na-Wo (which became Eagle Cove), Cascade (Cascade Lake), and Dart's Lake. Longstaff was certainly the most prolific camp founder of the Depression, but other aspiring camp directors also snapped up bargains. Mary Danzinger, a Kosher caterer from New York City, purchased Camp Algonquin at a tax sale in 1929. Her business took off when she attracted the children of the Bronfman family of Montréal, whose patronage gave the camp a good recommendation among prominent families in Québec's Jewish community.[S42] In 1936 Louis Lamborn, director of Camp Red Cloud in Brackney, Pennsylvania, purchased the former Camp Theodore Roosevelt, which had recently closed, and moved his camp to the Adirondacks.

Organized camping does not seem to have been among the most hard-hit Adirondack industries during the Depression. Probably camp attendance waned as families found they could not afford to send their children to camp. Camp Riverdale reduced the cost of a summer at camp during the 1930s, probably in an attempt to keep their customers. In the late 1920s the fee was $350. By 1933, the fee had fallen to $250, "a veritable bargain," as the catalog put it. In the $350 days, the usual enrollment was 60 boys; in 1933 only 33 boys came, and not all of them stayed for the entire season. Riverdale weathered the storm however, and by 1935 enrollment was up to 105.[S43]

Even if the total number of campers declined, there were still enough to keep most camps going. In 1925 at least 108 camps were operating in the Adirondacks; in 1935 the number was at least 94. There seem to have been enough children to sustain hope in the breasts of the camp leaders as well; in the 1930s at least twenty-two new camps were founded.[S44] The continued health of the camping industry was a boon to Adirondack residents. John Buyce, as mayor of Speculator, noticed it; the residents of Raquette Lake, where there were four children's camps in 1935, housing about three hundred children, noticed it. One longtime resident there, a former camp caretaker, feels that the camps kept the region's economy going.[S45]

Just as the Great Depression affected camping, so did World War II. Boys' camps had a particular problem because so many young men of counselor age left for the armed services. Some camps, like the Adirondack Music Camp (Upper Chateaugay Lake), closed altogether. Camp Horicon (Brant Lake) changed from a camp for boys—who presumably needed more supervision—to a camp for young men, because it had trouble finding counselors. Other camps instituted a "Counselor in Training" program in which older boys not old enough for the armed services performed as junior counselors. Mary Danzinger's Camp Algonquin had a more serious problem than lack of counselors. She closed the camp altogether during the war because the Canadians, a large part of her clientele, could not come to camp in the States.[S46] [HEB]

from the railway station to and from camp. They owned busses and were under contract to the school districts during most of the year, but late in June from the early 1920s until 1951 they met the special camp trains from New York City at the Riverside station. There were eight or ten coaches on each train, for two or three days in a row, carrying several hundred campers and their overnight bags destined for Camp Wakonda, the Brant Lake Camp, Camp Red Wing, and other camps in the area. The trunks arrived in baggage cars several days later and had to be distributed. In August, the whole process was reversed.[114] Caretaking at children's camps—putting in the docks in the spring, shoveling off the roofs in the winter, and all the tasks in between—was the most common job available to locals even

CAMP LAJEUNESSE, 1940

We are planning to have military training in 1941, as we did in 1917, and I am all for it, as I think we all need more discipline to awaken us to the responsibility of life. For the past ten years I have noticed a growing tendency to a lack of responsibility. I therefore think that a definite tightening up with more discipline and military training will help us all.[S47]

CAMP MINNOWBROOK, 1959

Our ways of life have changed, and with it our ideas on camping have been altered or expanded to meet the needs of the oncoming generations. The basic concept of a good camping experience still holds true. New needs have, however, arisen from our educational patterns in school and the interests cultivated in the home. They cannot be ignored during the eight weeks at camp.[S48]

though caretaking rarely has been a full-time occupation anywhere in the area.

"The Needs of the Oncoming Generations"

Organized camping survived the Depression and war intact as a distinct Adirondack institution. Over the following half-century, Adirondack camping developed in response to changes in American society. The social upheavals of the

1960s, the specialization of American education, and an increased awareness of the differences among children and their learning styles all had their effects.

After the Second World War, the nation experienced a period of prosperity that might have been expected to encourage a growth in Adirondack camping. There was indeed a small boom in camp foundation right after the war in which at least thirty camps were established. Only about forty were founded in the next nearly half-century, how-

Camp Eagle Cove baseball team, 1950. Courtesy of Joan Jacobs Brumberg.

CAMP GREYLOCK, 1960

Happy talk, keep talking happy talk
Talk about things Naomi likes
If it's not integration
It must be segregation
We'd rather go on an early nature hike![S49]

ever, nothing like the number begun in the prosperous years at the early part of the century. No doubt this difference is partly because of "camp saturation."

There were enough camps to go around in part because fewer families were choosing camp. For one thing, many parents no longer felt such an urgent need to get children out of the cities. Cities were becoming healthier places to live—or perhaps the American public was getting used to their "dust, dirt, and dangers." Air conditioning units practical for home use became available in the early 1950s, and almost at the same time an effective vaccination for polio was introduced. In addition, children at home in the

summer could participate in more organized activities than had been available before the war. Little League baseball, perhaps the prime example, was founded in 1939 and became very popular after the war. There were twelve leagues, all in Pennsylvania, when the war ended. Just two years later there were ninety-four leagues scattered all over the country. In 1949 the number of leagues nationally had jumped to 307.[115]

IN THE 1950s, well before feminism became a recognized phenomenon with the publication of Betty Friedan's *The Feminine Mystique,* two camps became leaders in encouraging young women to look beyond the home for their careers. Proponents of single-sex education had designed programs to enable women to achieve their full potential since the late nineteenth century, but there was a new intensity to the work of Sara Blum and Naomi Levine. Both Blum, who founded Camp Navarac in 1952, and Levine, who took over Camp Greylock in 1955, were prominent in Jewish political and philanthropic life. They encouraged girls to build well-rounded lives that included career, service, and family. Blum is remembered by her former

Archers at Camp Navarac, 1956. The Adirondack Museum, P66212.

campers for using *The Little Engine That Could,* the children's book by Watty Piper, as the basis of every final Sabbath service. Her theme was always the importance of perseverance and the ability of every woman to achieve daunting tasks. Levine steered girls toward more mature reading. All senior campers were expected to study their copies of the Sunday *New York Times* and to be prepared to discuss current events in the evening.

While camp directors like Naomi Levine and Sara Blum stuck staunchly by the ideal of single-sex education, most other new Adirondack camp leaders opted for coeducation. Almost four times as many camps founded in the postwar period were coeducational than were boys' camps.[116] Single-sex camps continued to exist and to attract campers, but some began to include the opposite sex in more activities than just dances and socials. Camps Lincoln and Whippoorwill, under the same management since 1931 but with separate programs and facilities for boys and girls, instituted a coed program in 1947. After the war at least a dozen camps changed their orientation completely, from a boys or girls camp to a coed camp.

At the same time modern feminism was being born in postwar prosperity, the modern evangelical movement was beginning. Fundamental Protestant organizations had been gathering strength out of the limelight ever since they were publicly discredited after the Scopes "Monkey Trial" in 1925. They grew dramatically in the 1950s and 1960s, using

Chapel at Camp Tapawingo on Lake Pleasant, 1970. The American Indian figure is the camp mascot, Wahonka. Courtesy of Camp Tapawingo at Camp-of-the-Woods.

Dance class at Camp Eagle Cove, 1950. Courtesy of Joan Jacobs Brumberg.

radio stations and Bible institutes as well as summer camps to spread their belief in the literal truth of the Bible.[117] The Word of Life Fellowship, a young organization dedicated to fundamentalist evangelism, purchased an island estate in Schroon Lake in 1946 for its youth camp. Word of Life expanded rapidly, purchasing the Brown Swan—a resort formerly patronized largely by Jewish vacationers and parents of neighboring campers—in 1952 for an adult camp. In 1955 it purchased Camp Rondack for another children's camp. In terms of numbers, the Word of Life camping venture was wildly successful. By 2000, between 6,400 and 8,000 teens and children were attending camp in Schroon Lake every summer.[118] Young Life, another fundamentalist organization that concentrated on youth ministry, was founded in Texas in 1941. Young Life entered the Adirondack camping business in 1969, purchasing the former Camp Navarac as one of its twenty-one youth camps across the country. By the end of the twentieth century, 3,300 teens

Fencing was taught at Moss Lake Camp, initially as preparation for tennis. The Adirondack Museum, P67514.

were spending a week at this camp, renamed Saranac Village, each summer.[119]

WHEN CAMP MINNOWBROOK DIRECTOR Paula Eppstein addressed the Association of Private Camps in 1959, she spoke of the need for children to keep up with more rigorous academics and "the interests cultivated in the home." By the time she spoke, specialization in both academic subjects and hobbies was several decades old in Adirondack camps. George Longstaff was a pioneer in specialization, advertising Camp Cedar Isles as a sailing camp when it opened in 1934. Like most other campers at specialty camps in the region through the end of the century, the Cedar Isles boys swam and worked on arts and crafts projects in addition to sailing. The camp program remained traditional; what had changed was the emphasis. Longstaff promoted the fact that campers concentrated on one particular skill that he felt would be useful later in life more than the general healthy outdoor life of camp.

Reveille at Camp Che-Na-Wah, ca. 1950, performed by a camper. Usually a bugle or trumpet was heard at reveille and taps each morning and night. Camps without musical staff might broadcast a recording over a loudspeaker system; those with particular talent used it. Tanager Lodge director Fay Welch was an accomplished musician who had played with the Syracuse Symphony in college; he woke campers and sent them to sleep with flute melodies. Courtesy of Ruth and Melvin Wortman, Camps Che-Na-Wah and Baco.

DEERWOOD ADIRONDACK MUSIC CENTER, 1952

Summer is the ideal time to develop artistically. Unhampered by the pressures of passing academic courses and by the amazing number of extra-curricular distractions, the Deerwood student can expose himself entirely to artistic challenges.[S50]

In the postwar period, more Adirondack camps specialized in one sport or discipline. After the war, campers could perfect their strokes at one of two swim camps—the Adirondack Swim Camp (Lake Lucretia), which opened in 1944 and was run by a physical education instructor from Rochester, and Meenagha Lodge, which started positioning itself as "the country's foremost aquatic camp" in 1946. By the 1960s Meenagha Lodge boasted aging Olympian and screen star Buster Crabbe on its faculty.

Bass and cello students at the New York State Music Camp, ca. 1950. Courtesy of Robert F. Swift.

At the Deerwood Adirondack Music Center adaptations of Adirondack lean-tos were used as practice studios. The Adirondack Museum Library.

Music camps seemed to fit naturally into the Adirondacks, perhaps because of the longstanding belief in the value of nature as artistic inspiration. Students at most Adirondack music camps spent much of the day in music study, but their schedules also included outdoor activities such as swimming and canoeing. Other camp traditions were sometimes included and adapted as well; at the Deerwood Adirondack Music Center reveille was sounded not by a sole bugler, but by a trumpet trio.

The Adirondack Music Camp on Chateaugay Lake, founded in 1934, was the first music camp in the region. When it closed during the Second World War because of

Baton twirling was offered at the New York State Music Camp in the 1950s. Courtesy of Robert F. Swift.

staffing shortages, Sherwood Kains, the musical director, moved to Saranac Lake and started the Deerwood Adirondack Music Center. Right after the war, in 1944, Ivan Galamian, a world-renowned violin teacher, opened the Meadowmount School of Music on a private estate near Westport. Meadowmount accepted students from eight up to thirty years of age, and is still in existence. The New York State Music Camp opened in the former Otter Lake Hotel on Fourth Lake in 1947. It outgrew its facility in 1955 and moved to Oneonta, where it still exists. Louis Roth closed his Stonegate Music and Arts camp after only a few seasons, but in 1969 David Katz, director of the Queens Symphony Orchestra, bought it and started what is now the Long Lake Camp for the Arts. From a musical beginning, the camp expanded by the 1990s to include instruction in all sorts of performing and fine arts, from pottery to circus skills.

The question of how "campy" to make camp particularly affected specialty camps whose directors had to choose between providing up-to-date facilities or fostering the closeness of the musician with nature. At Deerwood, practice studios were Adirondack lean-tos. Campers at the New York State Music Camp on Otter Lake had to isolate themselves from the warm summer Adirondack weather during their recording sessions for their radio broadcasts. They recorded in an uninsulated building with all the doors and windows tightly closed to keep out the noise of the camp. One camper likened the recording studio to a

Girls at the Moss Lake Camp learned classical ballet.
The Adirondack Museum, P43155.

sauna. When the session was over "campers would make a beeline for the lake, some without taking time to change to bathing suits."[120]

The "academic" type of summer camp, at which life skills other than woodcraft were taught as they might be in a city, was revived and intensified after the Second World War. George Longstaff declared that his Moss Lake Camp was distinguished from other camps because of "our efforts to provide technically accurate instruction for each girl in the activities which we feel will add most to the enjoyment of her future as well as her current happiness."[121] Longstaff had definite ideas about what skills girls would need as adults. The program at Moss Lake included swimming and diving, riding, sailing and canoeing, tennis, fencing, riflery, archery, dance, and crafts. Each of Longstaff's instructors was "a man whose life work is the specialty which he coaches at Moss."[122] Lothar and Paula Eppstein were also advocates of academic-type camping. The 1963 brochure for their Camp Minnowbrook read like a college catalog. Ninety-five different activities were listed in nine different categories (all taught by "highly trained specialists"), from "batique" (Art), to Rocketry (Nature and Science), with activities like ice skating, classical ballet toe work, theater makeup, construction of oscilloscopes, ear training, and speedboat driver training in between.[123]

Organized sports formed an important part of Adirondack camp programs since the Pok-O-Moonshine boys slid "onto" second base around the turn of the twenti-

Many of the summer-long camps with varied programs took
their campers on trips to cultural and historic sites as well as on
wilderness trips. In this 1958 photo, a group of Echo campers poses
on the Porter locomotive at the Adirondack Museum the year after
the museum opened. The Porter engine ran between Raquette Lake,
where the camp was located, and Utowana Lake from 1900 to
1929. The Adirondack Museum, P43155.

Photograph by Richard Walker

In the 1970s Lynx Camp began accepting girls. They participated in the same vigorous hiking and canoeing program as the boys. Courtesy of George Linck.

eth century. In the 1950s, with the popularity of camp specialization, camps provided a greater variety of sports and intensified sports training. Camp Eagle Cove responded to the popularity of Little League baseball by putting together its own league in the 1950s.[124] Camps dedicated to one sport had become very popular in urban America by the 1970s, but they remained rare in the Adirondacks. One reason for this is that sports camps require elaborate and specialized facilities most often found at colleges and universities, of which there are few in the Adirondacks. Camps—particularly boys' camps such as the Brant Lake Camp—continued to respond to the demand for more sports training, but the Lake Placid Soccer Camp, founded in 1976, was the only true sports camp.

As some camps shifted from woodcraft and nature study to academic subjects, other camps went the other way, concentrating on extensive hiking and canoe trips. Lynx Camp was founded by a physical education instructor from West Point Military Academy who was asked by a colleague to take the colleague's son on a canoe trip in Canada in the late 1940s. George Linck developed this trip into an organized program that was based on an island in Raquette Lake after 1966. Until the camp closed in 1978 the campers were rarely there, however. The island was used for learning skills and beginning-of-the-season shakedowns, but campers spent most of the summer going on canoe trips. The younger ones went out for a night or two; the oldest packed up their gear, loaded it onto trucks, and headed for

Canada.[125] The Adirondack Swim Camp reoriented and renamed itself "Swim and Trip" in the early 1960s when the founder's son took over. The program was based on long trips and hiking; campers could become "46ers" by the end of a full seven-year camp career.[126] Camp Riverdale, founded in 1912 as a Woodcraft camp with a strong tradition of canoe trips, closed in 1964. The following year it opened under new ownership and with a new name, The Adirondack Wilderness Camp. Gone were the glee club trips to Saranac Inn and the Woodcraft rituals; instead boys hiked into the trailless Seward Range for a week at a time. The totem poles remained, but were moved from the council ring to the main lodge.

Boy Scout camps never really lost their emphasis on wilderness travel. Scouts have taken trips from their base camps ever since Camp Russell was founded in 1918. By the 1970s the Scouts who were staying at the region's camps were joined by increasing numbers of nonresident Scouts, troops that came to the Adirondacks just to make a hiking or canoeing trip. Some of these troops were not well equipped or trained for a trek in the wilderness. The regional Association for Adirondack Scout Camps developed a training program for Scout guides, called Voyageurs, who would then be available to visiting troops. Voyageur-guided troops could also make use of the established Scout camps as bases and way-points. This Voyageur program became the basis of the national Scout Trek training program.[127]

New Voyageur Sarah Repak with instructor Keith Kelley at Lookout Point on Low's Lake, Sabattis Scout Reservation. Courtesy of Kristofer Alberga, Association of Adirondack Scout Camps.

RONDACK, CA. 1950

We had "services" on Saturday mornings. These were not about God, but rather, lectures by Mr. Chankin on topics he felt were important to young ladies . . . one that I remember was about the evils of chewing gum. We needed to sit up very straight and pay attention at these services or we would lose points for our teams![S51]

Jewish camping as it had existed in the Adirondacks since Isaac Moses came to Schroon Lake in 1906 began to disappear in the postwar period. Of the approximately twenty secular Jewish camps that remained after the Second World War, nine folded in the 1950s and 1960s. By the 1950s, Jews were no longer routinely excluded from camps patronized by Gentiles. The programs at Jewish camps like Schroon Lake, which closed in 1960, and Camp Severance, which ceased operation in 1970, had not been very different from their neighboring Gentile camps. The secular Jewish camp of the Adirondacks no longer necessarily had something different to offer.

Jewish families did find distinctly Jewish camps elsewhere in the Northeast, which is probably one reason Jewish camping declined in the Adirondacks. Jewish children in the 1950s and 1960s could choose from Conservative, Orthodox, Zionist, and even Yiddish camps in the Poconos, in the Catskills, and along the Hudson. At these camps, Jewish youth developed a sense of Jewish identity and community as well as studied their religion.[128] With the birth of the State of Israel in 1948, Judaism gained a new degree of legitimacy and Jews became more culturally assertive. A postwar religious revival, along with the arrival of Jewish youth workers from Europe, led to the establishment of more culturally and religiously Jewish camps in this country. They were mostly not in the Adirondacks, with its tradition of assimilated upper-class Jewish campers, but closer to larger population centers of more recently arrived Jewish families.

There was only one camp in the Adirondacks with a strong Jewish religious program after the Second World War. Camp North Star (also known as Star Lake) was founded about 1945 on a lake south of Malone and was out of business by 1962. The Orthodox camp kept kosher and had long services both Friday night and Saturday morning. The program otherwise seems to have been much like any other camp program at the time, however, with swimming, boating, and sports.

In the latter part of the twentieth century there were some efforts to make Adirondack camping more accessible to lower-income campers, but they were hampered by the distance from large numbers of eligible children. It was expensive to bus children from the New York metropolitan area or Boston to the region. The Warren County Children's Health Camp, established in 1922 for children who were at risk for tuberculosis, was the only camp wholly for underprivileged children, and it served only the local population.

Special needs children have also been scarce on the Adirondack camping scene, probably because of the distance of the Adirondacks from special services. Camp Triangle (McCauley Pond) was one of the few exceptions.

Friday night services at Camp Eagle Cove in the 1950s. Courtesy of Joan Jacobs Brumberg.

Building a lean-to at Camp Triangle, ca. 1965. Courtesy of Shirley Schofield.

Senior camper work crew from Camps Lincoln and Whippoorwill. By the time this photo was taken in about 1970, the two camps were under one management and known as The North Country Camps. Courtesy of North Country Camps.

Founded in 1957 to serve mentally retarded children, most of whom came from neighboring counties, it closed in 1990 largely because of the increasing burden of meeting state health regulations. In the late twentieth century, a few new special-needs camps opened, including a camp for children coping with grief, and the Double H--Hole in the Woods Camp near Lake Luzerne, a camp cosponsored by actor Paul Newman for seriously ill children. Some camps in the region developed short programs before or after their regular seasons for children with special needs. The Adirondack Woodcraft Camps run a camp for asthmatics in late August, and Camp Mark Seven (near Old Forge), a camp run by the Catholic Church with programs for adults, young people, and families dealing with hearing impairment, has a week exclusively for children.

ONE SUNDAY MORNING IN 1971, the boys of Camp Dudley were gathered at their outdoor chapel for the traditional Christian service. Junior leaders were often asked to read a passage from the Bible, and the designated reader this Sunday was African American. Instead of reading the Gospel, he shocked the mostly white, Christian congregation by refusing to continue to take part in a service that he felt had no relevance to blacks and people of other faiths.[129] The junior leader at Camp Dudley was only one of the many Americans questioning the form and philosophy of American institutions during the 1960s and 1970s. Camp leaders and campers alike reevaluated the regimentation, segregation of the sexes, and authority structure of so many children's camps, and camping changed in response.

Thirty-seven children's camps closed in the Adirondacks after 1960. No doubt some were felt to be old-fashioned and irrelevant. Others remained open and promoted their adherence to traditional values as an antidote to frightening change. Some, like Dudley, tackled the issues of the day head on. Rollie Stichweh, who had just been hired as director when the black leader stopped the chapel service, was a Vietnam veteran who had returned from duty questioning the war. The board of directors told him when they hired him that the camp was in difficulty; some campers and leaders were openly questioning camp customs such as the award system and the racially homogenous nature of the camp population, and expressing it by turning up at camp with long and unruly hair or insisting on a social life away from camp. "Stich" managed to pilot the camp through the turbulent 1970s in part by making judicious choices between change and continuity. He dealt with the hair issue by not making it an issue, and he actively recruited underrepresented groups as campers, helped in part by a large scholarship fund established by previous campers who had done well in the Establishment.[130] The

management of the Brant Lake Camp began involving its college-aged counselor staff more in planning meetings, rather than issuing directives about how the camp would be run.[131]

Many American Indian aspects of Adirondack camp life were casualties of the 1960s and 1970s. Indian activists were pointing out that regardless of the good intentions with which the Indian content had been adopted, the Indians were living peoples and not stereotypes to be used in play.[132] Camp Lincoln was one of the camps that quietly dropped much of its Indian content. For forty years, the campers had met weekly at a council fire. Everyone arrived in silence, wearing blankets, with the feathers they had been awarded for accomplishments stuck into leather headbands. A camp leader had started the fire itself with a bow drill, and the ritual that followed might have been outlined by Ernest Thompson Seton himself. Campers sang songs and presented skits and stories, and staff made new awards. As the counselor made each award the campers signified their approval by saying "How."[133] The council fire did remain at Lincoln, without the Indian symbolism but as the central ritual of camp.

Some camps kept their Indian rituals but altered and authenticated them. In the 1950s, the boys at Pok-O-Moonshine were divided into four tribes (Mohawks, Cayugas, Tuscaroras, and Senecas) for "that one special week that makes [this camp] unique," a Color War—like event called the Indian Games. The Great Indian Relay Race and Capture the Chief's Bonnet were standard events; in the

For over a century city parents have sent their children to camp in the Adirondacks to give them a close look at nature. This Echo camper became familiar with frogs in the 1950s. The Adirondack Museum.

"Playing Indian" at Adirondack Woodcraft Camps, ca. 1960. Courtesy of John Leach, Adirondack Woodcraft Camps.

"Young Fishermen" at Adirondack Woodcraft Camps, ca. 1960. The Adirondack Museum, P15938.

1970s Indian Skulking, Scalping, and Scavenging were added. By the end of the century the camp had expanded the Indian program. The chiefs, sachems, and storytellers of each of the camp tribes visited the Six Nations Iroquois Museum in Onchiota to learn about the American Indians on whose culture the camp games are modeled. The storytellers chronicled each aspect of the games in writing, and their journals were judged as part of games scoring.

ON APRIL 22, 1970, America celebrated the first Earth Day. Congress adjourned, students roamed their communities collecting garbage, and pedestrians took over city streets. The intent of Earth Day was to focus the nation's attention on abuse of the environment, but the effects also were felt in children's camps in the Adirondacks, an area symbolic of an untouched natural world.

After Earth Day, the New York State Department of Environmental Conservation reoriented the camps it had been running since the late 1940s. Camp Colby (Lake Colby) and Camp Raquette (Raquette Lake) had started as boys' camps with programs that introduced the department's work for sportsmen such as forestry and fish and game management. During the 1970s the camps went coed and tried to give the campers an appreciation of ecology and modern conservation.[134] Seventy years later, the department had rediscovered Ernest Thompson Seton's theory that "the subtleties of woodcraft" learned in childhood could result in an ecological perspective in adulthood.[135]

"Eleven Bumpy Miles from Nowhere"

Several million children have been to camp in the Adirondack region over the past century. Some stayed for a week, sleeping on a cot in a lean-to. Some stayed for two months, bunking in a stone cottage with a lake view. Some learned to aquaplane, some climbed a High Peak, some fell in love for the first time. Some claim they had the best summer of their lives; some were miserable.

Jokes about camp life abound—readers of a certain age will remember Alan Sherman's 1963 song "Camp Granada." Notwithstanding the images of poison ivy, lost campers, and ptomaine poisoning, the song ends with the camper enjoying himself. Over three thousand people have participated in the Adirondack Museum's children's camps

CHANGES IN AMERICAN FAMILY LIFE

In the Hayley Mills film The Parent Trap, *twin girls (both played by Mills) are sent to camp for the summer. Each lives with a different parent, and neither knows of the other's existence. After they find out who they are, they hatch a plan to get their parents back together. The plan is almost ruined because the father is about to get married again; we get the idea that he shipped his daughter off to camp to get her out of the way of his romance. The nuclear family is restored by the end of the film of course, this being a film from 1960. Divorce is now a fact of life for nearly half of the families in America forty years later, and is only one of several major changes in the American family that have affected organized camping.*

By 1970 nearly half of the women in America worked outside the home. They sent their children to a residential summer camp at least in part for childcare. But if camping may have gained campers at the end of its first century because of the need for summertime childcare, it may have lost campers to divorce. The divorce rate skyrocketed in the latter quarter of the twentieth century. A common arrangement in a divorced family with two custodial parents is for the child to live with one during the school year and the other during vacations. The vacation-parent often wants to be with the child, rather than send her or him off to camp. Another characteristic that modern families share, however, sometimes increases the importance of camp to those that stick with it. Modern families are often dispersed. Parents follow careers and don't necessarily live close to their siblings and parents. For many of the long-standing private camps, and even some of the long-lived organizational camps, a summer at camp becomes something the different generations and the different parts of the family have in common.[S52] [HEB]

CAMP GREYLOCK, 1960

I have often wondered why children should fall in love with a place that is 11 bumpy miles from nowhere, that has no showers in the bunks, no TV, a telephone that rarely works, a canteen that sells only bobby pins and kotex (no soda pop or ice cream), a temperamental generator, and an impossible director.

First, I think that the physical setting of the camp, its location and site play a key role in the creation of this mood. Even the most indifferent child cannot help but react to the natural beauty of the Raquette Lake area. Its magnificent sunsets, its beautiful blue waters, its impressive star-studded nights and its wild isolation—all produce a feeling of removal from the pressures and problems of living. It produces a feeling of almost idyllic retreat. I think that adults fail to realize how many pressures we put on children and that childhood is not all roses and honey. I think a retreat from these pressures in an atmosphere that seems millions of miles away from TV, telephones, streamlined highways and hot showers produces a feeling of peace and contentment. And I think that one gets attached to a place that can produce this feeling.[S53]

study, and nearly all were positive about their camp experience. Certainly people who had good memories of camp were more likely to be interested in the study and to be enthusiastic about sending comments than those who hated camp, but the evidence strongly suggests that many children who attended Adirondack children's camps were indeed "happy campers."

It could hardly be otherwise. Most of the campers have been urban children transported to a new and exciting environment. They are on their own, most of them, for the first time in their lives, and many of the rules of everyday life are suspended. At the private camps especially, children are surrounded by a large staff—many of whom are not so very old themselves—whose business it is to make sure they have a good time. Camp leaders have always been concerned that children enjoy themselves at camp. After all, unlike most conventional educational institutions, if the children don't have a good time at camp they don't have to come back.

In addition to making sure the children have a good time, however, camp leaders ever since Sumner Dudley, Ernest Thompson Seton, and the Progressive educators have taken seriously the educational goals of camp. They have striven to teach self-reliance and how to live responsibly and kindly with others. They have taught swimming and canoeing, batik and trapeze. With examples and en-

The inscription on this photo, taken on Parent's Weekend at Camp North Star in 1962, reads, "I didn't want my parents to leave." Courtesy of Patricia Richards.

Storytime at Schroon Lake Camp, ca. 1940. Courtesy of the Schroon-North Hudson Historical Society.

couraging words they have tried to mold and reward good character. With charts, badges, and honor awards they have assessed the impact camp has had on the campers.

The camping movement has had unintended consequences as well. Chief among these is the effect on the Adirondack economy, which has been significant, but probably not as much so as other summer tourist industries. Like many other parts of the seasonal economy in the Adirondacks, children's camps depend largely on capital from outside. Rather more than most other seasonal industries, however, they also depend primarily on workers from outside the region. Directors and counselors, by and large, have not been drawn from the local population. They have traditionally been college students or professional educators studying or working elsewhere during the rest of the year. Even many service jobs—like those of the cooks James

Hankins and Mary Smedley—often went to outsiders. In the past two decades counselors and support staff are increasingly foreign students looking for a paid visit to the United States—from a different "outside," but still "outside."

"CAMP GRANADA"

Hello Muddah, hello Fadduh,
Here I am at Camp Granada.
Camp is very entertaining,
And they say we'll have some fun if it stops raining.
. . . .
Wait a minute, it stopped hailing,
Guys are swimming, gals are sailing.
Playing baseball, gee that's betta,
Muddah, Fadduh, kindly disregard this letter![S54]

Caretaker at Adirondack Woodcraft Camps, ca. 1940. Courtesy of John Leach, Adirondack Woodcraft Camps.

The job of camp caretaker has traditionally been local and largely remains so. Just like owners of private family camps and second homes, camp directors need someone on the spot year-round to shovel off the roofs in winter, put the docks in and take them out, and generally maintain the buildings. Other service jobs around camp have increasingly gone to outsiders, however. In the first part of the twentieth century local people like the guides Sauseville and Ryan at Dudley and Pok-O-Moonshine worked in children's camps. Camps no longer hire guides, and local workers often choose to take other, longer-term jobs. Most camps, as seasonal operations, cannot afford to provide the benefits and long-term work available from many of the other low-skilled jobs in the region. Laundry workers and kitchen help have sometimes been recruited locally, but just as often the jobs have been given to former campers who wanted to spend another year or two at camp, or to campers as a form of scholarship.

The biggest financial impacts of camps on the Adirondack economy are indirect. Private, for-profit camps contribute to the tax base—$13,295,832 for the whole state in 1996.[136] Most camps run by not-for-profit organizations, like the Scouts and religious organizations, do not pay taxes. This fact has led to some hard feelings on the part of local residents, who do pay taxes, part of which goes toward services for the campers. This resentment is especially noticeable in a region where even the state makes payments in lieu of taxes on state-owned property. The YMCA's Camp Dudley and the religious group Young Life's camp on Upper Saranac Lake are particularly high-profile examples of not-for-profit camps that have tackled the question of their contributions to the local tax base. Dudley turns its extensive playing fields over to the local school district during the fall and spring and makes annual contributions to the town of Westport; Young Life makes annual contributions to the Upper Saranac Lake Association and the Town of Santa Clara.

Today, in the early twenty-first century, visiting parents are the most visible impact of camping on the Adirondack economy. Camp visitors—parents and children—spent $60,627,033 on transportation, food, lodging, shopping, and entertainment throughout the state in 1996. Motels in towns near camps are booked up well in advance for the beginnings and endings of camp sessions at both private and organizational camps, and for parents' visiting weekend at the larger private camps.

Children's camping and the Adirondack Park grew up together. The Park was established the same year that Sumner Dudley first brought his boys to the region, at a time when Forest Preserve legislation, which prohibited logging on all state lands, had been in place for almost a decade. By the 1970s regulations governing the Park kept development restrained and preserved large tracts of public land. The result has been that the natural environment of children's camping has changed much less in the Adirondacks than it has almost anywhere else in the Northeast.

A SPECIAL advertising section of the *New York Times Magazine* on 2 March 2003 opened, "SPANISH. SCUBA. SOCCER. SATs. With summer camp and school directors working harder than ever to please today's kids, anyone can have a great summer experience." There is a soccer camp in the Adirondacks, and campers at another camp can learn scuba diving in a cold Adirondack lake. Most Adirondack children's camps today are what the *New York Times* would call "traditional camps." Even if they do teach scuba and Spanish, they leave time in their schedules for boating, swimming, and just being in the woods. The land use regulations of the Adirondack Park that protect the wild character of the region have sustained traditional camping here. Many camps elsewhere in the Northeast are finding that they no longer provide such a clearly different setting than the camper's homes and that it is more difficult to maintain programs that depend on the natural environment.[137]

Caretaker Dean Pohl helps director Frances Clough out of the camp launch Echo *about 1950. The Adirondack Museum.*

A Lynx Camp trip, ca. 1965. Courtesy of George Linck.

Organized camping in the Adirondacks has had an unintended consequence that is harder to measure than how well a child can paddle a canoe or how many dinners the hotel sells on parents' weekend. Even the camps where children spent most of their time learning to play tennis or edit videos seem to have given their campers an outdoor experience that stays with them all their lives.

For some campers, this is a deep love for the Adirondack region itself. This love for the Adirondacks has had a lasting impact on the region's economy and future. People who learned to love the region at camp and return to vacation or to buy second homes contribute to the enormously important seasonal economy of the region. Even those who never return may become an important constituency for the region. This population can be significant if they stay in the state and vote. Adirondack land-use planning and con-servation must be responsive to the public because of the laws governing development and use of the land in a park where people also live.

Other campers acquire a simple awareness of the natural world in their summer in the Adirondacks. The sound of the wind in the pines, the sensation of diving into a mountain lake on a hot day, or an expansive view with no sign of people in it can create that awareness in subtle and lasting ways. The enduring contribution of organized camping in the Adirondacks may be simply that "constant source of wonder and of learning" that Frank Hackett found in the natural world around Camp Riverdale in 1932.[138]

CAMP NAZARETH

Some city folks might say Camp Nazareth had limited resources. I believe it utilized its Adirondack setting, the greatest resource in N.Y., to provide its campers with a wealth of knowledge about the outdoors, the skills to embrace it, and the makings of lifelong memories.[555]

Tanager Lodge, ca. 1990. Courtesy of Tanager Lodge.

3 *"A Wiser and Safer Place"*

Organized Camping During World War II

IN LATE JULY 1943, as American troops fought their way up the Italian peninsula in Europe and moved northward in the Pacific through the Solomon Islands after the critical victory at Guadalcanal, a thirty-four-year-old school-teacher named Sidney Jacobs canoed across Raquette Lake in the heart of the Adirondacks.* He glided through the water for almost a mile from Raquette Lake Boys' Club to the Antlers, a resort on the mainland, just a mile off Route 28. It was almost dark, but the canoeist had made the same trip many times before that summer, in exactly the same way.

At the Antlers, he would rendezvous, as planned, with his wife, Frances, who was working as a counselor at the sister camp just outside Raquette Lake village. The two would stay the night in a room reserved for their use, and then they would each go back to their respective camps: Sid to the Boys Club where he was the head counselor; Fran to the Girls Club where she was in charge of a cabin of eight-year-old girls, each with long braids reconfigured every morning in the style of Hollywood's favorite child star, Margaret O'Brien. Sid and Fran Jacobs were my father and mother, and I was conceived on one of those starry nights on Raquette Lake, in the midst of World War II.

My father, a 1932 graduate of Syracuse University, had courted my mother for a number of years—longer than she wished—but they did not marry until December 1940 be-

cause of the difficulties of finding a secure teaching job during the Depression. A year later, like all Americans, their lives were changed by the Japanese attack on Pearl Harbor.

My father was teaching high school history in Mount Vernon, New York, when the war started. In 1934, he had earned a masters degree from Columbia Teachers College, where, along with history and economics, he took courses in progressive education and camp management. In the summers of 1938 and 1940, he was head counselor at Camp Tioga in Lake Cuomo, Pennsylvania, a job secured through the recommendation of a fellow teacher who worked at a nearby girls' camp. In the summers of 1939 and 1941, he ran Conestoga Trails, a traveling camp for boys. My father, two other teachers, and twenty-five boys, most of them from Westchester County, crossed the country from New York to California in three Woody station wagons, sleeping in traditional campsites as well as less orthodox locations such as football stadiums, municipal jails, Salvation Army headquarters, and a Civilian Conservation Corps camp. I remember him telling me what fun it was to unroll your sleeping bag, lie down, and look up at the stars from the fifty-yard line in the center of Schoelkopf Stadium at Cornell University in Ithaca, New York—where I have taught for close to twenty five years—but also in the massive, glamorous Rose Bowl in Pasadena. As a form of introduction on the road, my father carried with him a letter from

---

*A version of this article was given as a lecture entitled "A Safer and Wiser Place: Children's Camping During World War II" at the Adirondack Museum, Blue Mountain Lake, New York, on 21 July 2003. The lecture accompanied the opening of the exhibition A Paradise for Boys and Girls: Adirondack Children's Camps, which ran though 2006. Joan Jacobs Brumberg was a historical consultant on that exhibit. All of the quotations in this article are from *Camping Magazine,* 1942–45.

Sidney and Pricilla Anne Snell arrive at Camp Niaweh, near Warrensburg, about 1943. Courtesy of Sidney Anne Snell Fulford.

the mayor of Mount Vernon and the local police chief. The camp program was an intentional mix of sightseeing, education in American values, and work: in Kansas, the Westchester boys stopped to detassel corn for a week in order to see what agricultural labor was really like.

When my father was rejected by the army in early 1942 (he was classified 4F because of an active ulcer), he took on civil defense responsibilities in Mount Vernon, but his education and professional experience, his athleticism, and a longstanding love of the outdoors made him a perfect person to answer the call for wartime service in children's camping. Within weeks of the outbreak of war, the American Camping Association realized that they would face deep staff shortages in the summer of 1942. By the spring, dozens of ads for counselors ran in the *New York Times* clas-

sified section. Because so many young men were enlisting in the armed services, children's camps began to look for staff in unusual places—among retirees, refugees, foreign exchange students, members of the Junior League, and also the American Story Teller's Association. And because of their alleged special talents, directors were urged to open their doors, to consider "colored leadership for music and Japanese citizens for crafts." Camps that were historically staffed by men hired some women, and the push began to train teenagers sixteen and older as CITs, counselors-in-training.

My father was a plum of a hire because of his experience. In June 1942, as soon as the school year ended, he left home for Raquette Lake Boys' Club without my mother, a bride of only six months. Having a husband at camp was not like having a husband overseas, but it was still a separation that made my mother unhappy. The following year, in 1943, as the labor shortage intensified, both my parents went to work on Raquette Lake in order to take care of other people's children. It was a dislocation they were willing to endure for the war effort, and both felt good about pitching in.

By 1942, considerable attention had already been given to the role of camping in the national emergency. In both 1942 and 1943, camp directors met across the country to discuss what it meant to run camps for children while the nation was fighting a war for survival. The American Camping Association (ACA) meetings in these years were serious and pragmatic, as camp directors considered how to respond to the prospect of air raids and sabotage, shortages of labor and goods, new government restrictions, and the emotional and psychological needs of youngsters made anxious by what they saw and felt in the society around them.

The push for "preparedness" went hand in hand with a

"CAMPING FORWARD," 1943

Camping Forward! America's at war!
We pledge our resources to the cause we're fighting for;
While camping in the forests, the plains or by the sea
Respond to the summons for the cause of liberty![51]

new sense of vulnerability. Camp directors discussed practical strategies for protecting campers in case of air raids, camouflaging camp buildings from the air, and training children to cook outdoors in streets and vacant lots in case of large urban disasters. There were rumors of discussions in Washington that children's camps might be used in the event of mass evacuations from East Coast cities. In 1942, the ACA magazine *Camping* provided information on "evacuee camping" in case that scenario developed. From across the Atlantic, well-known psychiatrists and psychologists such as Anna Freud and John Bowlby argued against removing American children from their homes, basing their opinion on their experience with thousands of children who were evacuated from London during the Blitz. The English reported that sudden removal from home and separation from family produced severe depression in children.

Although every institution in American life—schools, churches, unions, corporations—had to map out its own unique part in the war effort, camping posed a special problem because of the frightening role of youth camps in the National Socialist success in Germany. In newsreels, newspapers, and magazines, Americans were exposed to images of blond, blue-eyed German youth demonstrating their physical strength, showing off their survival skills in the outdoors, and marching in crisp precision to honor their Führer. In 1938, Erika Mann, daughter of author Thomas Mann, published *School for Barbarians,* a widely reviewed book that laid out the process through which schools and camps were used by the Nazis to enforce the power of the state. In the same year, a Princeton University professor of politics, Harwood L. Childs, published a translation of *The Nazi Primer,* the bible of the Hitler Youth movement. By the early 1940s, many Americans were familiar with the ways in which National Socialism, youth camps, and militarism were intertwined.

In 1942, Governor Harold Stassen of Minnesota—a state with many children's camps—wrote, "We know the totalitarian countries have had camps for youth—camps in which youth was regimented, brought in under definite orders, young minds perverted into thinking, an attitude that would satisfy the wishes of dictatorial leaders, which would prepare them to become cogs in a ruthless machine." Governor Leverett Saltonstall of Massachusetts—another state

where camps were an important business—was more succinct: "In Europe, camps are the instruments of dictators to create more slaves."

Despite this frightening dimension, the model of fascist youth camps actually had some appeal to camp directors who worried that American children did not seem to be as "fervent" about their national ideals as those who marched beneath the swastika. As a result, some called for less recreation at summer camp and more emphasis on physical fitness, survival skills, and even regimentation and indoctrination in American values. While use of the word "indoctrination" made many in the camping community uneasy, others felt that it was exactly the right concept for the exigencies of the moment.

In a dialogue about the way wartime camping could foster national values, one director asked pointedly, "Does this mean that we are to use camping as a means to indoctrinate children with a particular point of view?" And then he answered his own question: "If we *all* believe in one big idea as a people [that] is essential to our existence as a nation, then definitely 'Yes.' " "Camping," he concluded, "is an instrument of the society it serves. As an agency for youth, it cannot dodge its primary responsibility of conditioning youth so that they can live successfully the type of life expected of them, in the nation [of] which they are a part."

By 1943, camping was being touted as a particularly effective antidote to fascist ideals by a host of well-known Americans. In addition to Stassen and Saltonstall, there was

Morning exercise at Camp Red Wing (Schroon Lake) had a militaristic look to it in 1925. The regimentation of some camps provoked fears of American camps becoming like Nazi youth camps. The Adirondack Museum.

Charles W. Eliot, director of the National Resources Planning Board, and first lady Eleanor Roosevelt. Approximately six weeks after Pearl Harbor, Mrs. Roosevelt gave an address at the Astor Hotel in Manhattan entitled "Children's Camping as I See It." She urged people not to call off camps in the summer of 1942 and counseled business as usual, acknowledging, of course, that the times were very unusual. Mrs. Roosevelt claimed to "have a great fondness for camping" (although no one was quite sure when she had ever done any), and she urged those in the field to find ways to broaden the base of American camping so that all children, regardless of social class and income, "should have this opportunity to benefit from nature."

The general concern seemed to be that if the Germans could use camping as a vehicle for building cultural cohesion, Americans could and should do the same—although the end goals would look very different. In the United States, camping would be used to foster the democratic state, a nation where people of different races and creeds worked together cooperatively. One longtime member of the ACA, Boyd Bode, explained in a 1942 article:

A cultural heritage must command the loyalty and devotion of the young people, if it is to have strength. For some reason or other, our young people are lacking in deep convictions and abiding loyalties. They do not know in any significant sense what they believe. It is not their fault. Their confusion springs from the confusions that reside in our cultural heritage. [Today] the central task of all education is indubitably to clarify our democratic tradition so that it may have the same kind of simplicity and power as the doctrines of totalitarianism in the dictatorship countries.

In the midst of an unprecedented national emergency, leaders of the American camping movement tried to do exactly that. Wartime camp directors were instructed to expand on historic traditions in American camping, but to give them a new twist. In addition to the standard fare—nature lore and crafts, swimming and boating, bonfires and singing—the ideal wartime camp needed to be a microcosm of democracy in action. Whether it was in the bunk or in the dining room, on the ball field or in a canoe, camp activities were now a venue for decision-making, cooperation, and demonstrations of responsible leadership. Camp was no longer about rugged individualism; it was about living in a group. The very best camp programs were designed

Camp Dudley published "Dear Chief: Excerpts from letters written to Chief by Dudley boys in service," a pamphlet of letters from former campers fighting in World War II who credited Camp Dudley with teaching them skills that helped them get through the war. Courtesy of Camp Dudley, YMCA Inc.

to foster collaborative projects and patriotism, values that America needed.

In wartime camping, all children had to pitch in regardless of their age. Before December 1941, American campers were already involved in a program called "Young America Wants to Help." At ninety-six American camps, campers picked berries and ran arts and crafts sales in order to raise money for European war relief. They also

Flag raising and lowering ceremonies had been a part of camp life before the war, as at Camp Agaming, pictured here in 1931. Teaching patriotism became even more important during the war. The Adirondack Museum.

went without meat and desserts so that camp owners could save money and contribute to the fund.

Once the United States was a full participant in the war, these efforts expanded beyond raising money, buying bonds, and collecting cans. For adolescent campers in particular, the war brought real responsibility in the form of work that was challenging but also fun. Teenagers cleared trails and marked out canoe routes; reported forest fires and spotted planes; learned map reading, weather reporting, telegraphy, and signaling; received basic education in equipment repair, motor mechanics, and construction; and assisted in local communities whenever there were shortages of adults. Adolescent boys were encouraged to "intensify personal hobbies," such as meteorology, astronomy,

Teaching practical skills such as auto mechanics gained new importance during the war although some camps, like Camp Lincoln (pictured here in 1925), already included them in their programs. Courtesy of North Country Camps.

CAMP UNDERCLIFF, 1945

One day in the dining hall, someone announced that Germany had surrendered and the war was over, and everybody ran down to the lake and jumped in.[52]

pioneering, and training carrier pigeons, expertise considered useful in wartime. Girls knit for soldiers and assisted with community blood banks. The theory was that America's children would both acquire lifelong skills and also gain personal satisfaction knowing they were helping with the war effort.

Ideas about the satisfactions of youthful hard work reflected prevailing theories of Progressive education, namely the value of learning by doing, but there was also a deep strain of antimaterialism provoked by the realities of wartime sacrifice: "For the duration, the American people are seeking values. Our education has helped us to know the price of everything and the value of nothing."

In this climate, wartime camp directors were deliberate about teaching patriotism. During the war years, there was more than just fireworks, hot dogs, and displays of the Stars and Stripes on the Fourth of July. Campers performed

At Moss Lake Camp, girls were divided into two teams. Membership was meant to convey a sense of belonging and an interest in teamwork. Leadership of a team was an honor reserved for senior girls. This is an induction ceremony about 1945. The Adirondack Museum, P43541.

plays and pageants extolling the virtues of the founding fathers and the spirit of a free people who refused to truck with tyranny. Whenever possible, campfires and rainy-day cabin programs were turned into educational opportunities about the settlement of America and the pioneer ethic. Instead of the old idea that liberty was the absence of restraint, liberty was redefined as "the opportunity for the progressive enrichment, intellectually, socially and esthetically of our everyday lives." And directors made systematic efforts, in the tradition of the New Deal's Works Progress Administration, to involve campers with the traditions and indigenous culture of the region where the camp was located. At barn dances, sing-alongs, plays, and ethnic festivals, youngsters from affluent city and suburban homes were expected to mix with locals, not simply for fun, but for enlightenment in the ways that "other" Americans lived.

The best-known advocate of this kind of red-white-and-blue camping was Paul Vories McNutt, a household name during the war because he served as federal security administrator and chairman of the War Manpower Commission. McNutt, a former Democratic governor of Indiana, began his service to the Roosevelt administration in 1939. Known as the "mobilizer-in-chief," he was on the cover of *Time, Newsweek,* and *Look* during the war years. He was also the person most closely associated with the "politics of margarine," a controversial wartime food product that put a knife into the heart of the dairy industry.

In June 1942, as American parents worried about whether or not to separate from their children during the first summer of a world war, McNutt assured them, "I do not know of a wiser or safer place for your children to be this summer than in an American summer camp." In addition to the good he did the camping business with that remark, McNutt also provided camp directors with an idealized model of the American summer camp. "Our camps today are small communities where each child learns democratic government by living it," he commented in "Children's Camping in Wartime," an article in the June 1942 issue of *Camping.* "Money and social position have no value here. The right to respect is earned only by what the child contributes by service to the success of his community."

Although American camps were, in fact, generally structured by social class and religion, McNutt was lavish in his praise for the American camping enterprise. In October

Paddling a war canoe—or just launching it—took teamwork and cooperation, important values during the war. The Adirondack Museum, P43821.

1942, he told a joint meeting of the ACA and at least a dozen federal agencies involved with the camp business:

We now know that camp life, be it but for two weeks, gives to boys and girls a training in self-reliance, utilization of skills, love of nature and the outdoors that no other institution in American life so adequately provides . . . [At camp] they learn to stand on their own, to be physically fit, to do hard things and do them well. They know that accomplishing difficult things makes for strong bodies and stalwart characters. They learn how to sacrifice and to serve, how to take orders as well as how to give them, how to follow as well as to lead and direct. They develop a capacity for cooperation and the sense of comradeship. They learn what a precious thing it is to *belong*. All of this would be valuable enough in peacetime. In wartime, camp life is a God-send.

Rhetoric like McNutt's contributed to the idea that camping was important, and it made camp directors, who were small business people as well as educators, willing to endure the significant economic challenges entailed in keeping camps open during the war. Although some camps did close, most survived, enduring a tangled web of government regulations and new requests from parents, including paying by installment and lowering tuition. *Camping* magazine admitted that the war challenged the business side of camping but that most directors felt that they had to "take it on the chin with the rest. To do so [was] a patriotic duty."

In his role as head counselor at Raquette Lake Boys Club, my father discovered almost immediately that transportation would be a problem for staff and campers. Because rubber was a necessity in both land and air military campaigns, it was in short supply, forcing camps to be conservative in their use of cars and trucks as well as sports equipment such as basketballs and tennis balls. When the Office of Defense Transportation, generally known as the ODT, mandated a reduction in tire mileage and greater usage of "common carriers"—regularly scheduled buses and trains—the trip to camp changed dramatically. Those leaving New York City for the Adirondacks or the Berkshires no longer drove in individual cars, and many campers were denied the ritualized pleasure of specially chartered camp buses. The ODT and the ACA, working together, suggested many schemes for making travel to and from camp more efficient. In addition to using common

carriers, directors considered staggering the opening, closing, and change days; lengthening the camp season; making long-distance hauls in relays; and using more primitive forms of transport, including the horse and buggy or hay wagons. Some even proposed that campers and staff hike to camp, with overnight stays in campgrounds or hostels along the way.

My parents were lucky: in the first summer of the war, they arranged a ride from Westchester County to the Adirondacks, but the trip took two full days, with a stop in the Cherry Valley, because the New York State Thruway did not yet exist. During the season, camp directors had to be inventive, and, just like everyone else, they had to apply for tires for their camp vehicles at their local ODT board. The ACA described the situation bluntly: "The ODT believes in summer camps but it aims to save rubber. Camping cannot expect a blank check from the government."

The same was true with food. By the summer of 1943, rationing was a fact of life. Each family member was issued ration books, and it was the challenge of the American homemaker to combine the stamps in the book and plan meals within set limits. Sugar, butter, coffee, and beefsteak were especially scarce and points were assigned to canned, bottled, and dehydrated fruits and vegetables in addition to meats and dairy products. Managers of children's camps had to find a way to handle the challenge of feeding large groups of youngsters three nutritious meals a day and also deal with the complexities of collecting and using the stamps in each child's ration book. By law, parents were required to turn them over to the camp management. Years

The girls of Silver Lake Camp go for a hayride and picnic for the Fourth of July, 1941. The Adirondack Museum.

later, my father told me that some parents forgot, but there were kids who came to camp carrying a half-pound of white cane sugar for every week they would be away from home. (This was the national per-person ration.)

With some annoyance, my father also told me about the headaches associated with the dreaded Form R1307—"Registration of Institutional Users"—for camps, like Raquette Lake Boys' Club, that had over fifty people. The R1307 provided complicated formulas for calculating the expected number of meals to be served during a season, but it also required camp directors to submit records of previous usage, especially when requesting items of high point value, such as bacon and fruit juice concentrate, both popular with campers. Some of the larger camps also used the Ration Banking Plan, in which their directors were authorized to remove a certain number of stamps from the ration books of campers and then deposit them at the local Ration Board where a ration point bank account was established. A director could then write checks against these ration points when he needed food supplies.

The wartime system was a formidable challenge requiring both accounting skills and nutritional knowledge. Advance registration of campers became a necessity, as did careful, constant food planning. Directors, with the advice of professional home economists and dieticians, experimented with creative ways to make use of leftovers, develop public storage such as refrigeration lockers, and substitute dehydrated and concentrated foods for perishable foodstuff. Camp gardens were touted everywhere as the best way to supplement shortages. Not only did gardens save money, they brought some diversity to a boring wartime diet heavy with beans and potatoes. It was a time of "thin sandwiches," both my parents recalled, when butter was usually diluted and cream cheese was combined with just about everything possible: jelly, olives, cucumbers, nuts, raisins, relish, mayonnaise. When wild strawberries, blueberries, and raspberries grew on or near camp grounds, wartime campers were unabashedly encouraged to find and consume these fruits of the earth because they were free and high in vitamins.

Challenged by the logistics of wartime management, camp directors still made the mental health of children a core concern. Paul McNutt warned about the "psychological dangers" faced by American children in wartime:

Camp gardening programs begun in the 1930s, such as this one at Silver Lake, served camps well during the war. The Adirondack Museum.

Parents for the most part are busily engaged in war production; they have sons in the armed forces; they are tense and worried and earnest. The children know it and react to it because children are quick to sense any anxiety adults may face. They are upset because they do not fully understand the national danger, the seriousness of it, and how to escape it. We cannot afford to have our children grow into hyperemotional men and women. We cannot permit the war to upset mental stability and natural growth.

The challenge for those who constituted what Tom Brokaw has dubbed "The Greatest Generation" was to keep wartime's emotional stress at a minimum. To that end, directors told both campers and staff to leave their radios at home "so as to eliminate the undesirable aspects of the news and the propaganda." Newspapers were not cut off, but staff was instructed to destroy them after they were read, rather than pass them around. And at the table and in the bunk, counselors were encouraged to "studiously avoid all war talk" and sing instead. Even parents were requested to refrain from war discussions in their letters or in their conversations on visiting day. *Camping* magazine stated with authority: "Pediatricians and psychologists will verify the value of a few weeks in the seclusion of a good summer camp."

Between 1942 and 1945, camping was reconceived as a retreat, a place where adults took special precautions, if not covert action, to shield children from the real world. This was a job that my father and mother, like many adults, took quite seriously. My parents went to camp again in the summer of 1943, this time armed with books and games, craft

Adirondack children's camps were far from the anxiety of war, none more so than those without road access, such as Tanager Lodge. Here, a group of young campers is ready for a canoe trip about 1945. Courtesy of Tanager Lodge.

materials and puzzles, plus a host of ideas about what to do in inclement weather, a reality in most Adirondack summers.

On rainy days, when the fog was thick and the carpet of golden pine needles in front of the cabins sloppy and soft, my father led campers in round robin stories and arranged quiz shows packed with silly riddles and puns. He also loved to sing, mostly songs with easy, rhyming words that even the youngest children could memorize and belt out, especially when it came to a chorus that was repeated over and over and over. To this day, I remember the wacky lyrics to "The Billboard Song," a lengthy ditty filled with names that kids in the l950s were unlikely to know but were willing to repeat anyway. My father started us out: As I was walking down the street a billboard met my eye; / The advertisements pasted there could make you laugh and cry. / The wind and rain had come that night and washed it all away, / And what was left upon that board would make the billboard say—" At this point, we campers chimed in: "Come smoke a Coca-Cola, chew ketchup cigarettes, / See Lillian Russell wrestle with a box of oysterettes." (My bunk eventually changed the name to Marilyn Monroe.) There were more faux advertising slogans in the song, none of which made any sense: "Castoria cures the measles." "Bay rum is good for horses." But that was exactly why we loved singing them so much.

Although only about 5 percent of American children actually went to camp during World War II, and most were the sons and daughters of the privileged class, those who did were taken care of by adults who were animated by a sense of immediacy and importance. "We can't just be counselors [this year]," a director wrote in 1942, "We have our destiny before us—to prepare the youth of today for the task of tomorrow. Therein lies our duty to God and our Country." McNutt, always the cheerleader for American camping, declared in 1943 that the United States had the "best equipped corps of camp directors and counselors existing anywhere in the world." Like Mrs. Roosevelt, he wanted to see camping become more egalitarian as a result of the war, but this was a promise left unfulfilled.

By the time the war ended on VJ Day in August 1945, I was walking and playing on the fine sand beach at the Antlers Hotel where my mother and I were guests of Max and Rose Berg, owners of the Raquette Lake camps. We had come to visit my father as he completed yet another summer as head counselor at the Boys Club. In 1946, he returned again without us, but in 1947 and 1948, we went with him to Camp Northwood in Remsen, New York, where he became the program director. In 1949, when I was five, he began a thirty-year association with Camp Eagle Cove on Fourth Lake in the Fulton Chain, part of a distinc-

Joseph (Bello) Snyder (left), director, and Sidney Jacobs, program director, Camp Eagle Cove, ca. 1950. Courtesy of Joan Jacobs Brumberg.

tive necklace of connected lakes that meanders through the Adirondacks from Old Forge to Saranac Lake.

In truth, until I was twenty-one years old and about to marry, I never thought about spending a summer anywhere else but in the Adirondacks, at camp. For all those years, there was nothing more exciting than the day at the end of June when I boarded the train out of Grand Central with all the other "New York kids" and traveled up the Hudson and along the Erie Canal to the grand Victorian train station at Utica, and then on to the tiny one at Thendara. There we were picked up by either a traditional yellow school bus rented from the Town of Webb, or the open, dark green Camp Eagle Cove truck, used also to haul garbage.

Almost all of us preferred the truck, so there was much discussion on the train about who would be lucky enough to ride in it. As we traveled on the South Shore Road along Fourth Lake and came closer and closer to camp, we sang in anticipation of our arrival, ignoring the truck's rank odor, and screamed wildly at every bend and bump in a road that cut through thousands of quiet acres of dense pine forest. It was a half-hour of pure exhilaration, probably impossible for my grandchildren to experience today because of laws intended to keep them safe and also because of the fear of litigation on the part of contemporary camp directors.

In the 1950s, when camp was not in session, I trailed along with my father to the American Camping Association conventions in New York City. This was always a special occasion for me because I wore my camel's hair coat and patent leather Mary Janes, and carried a small shopping bag. Bored by the speeches and panels that my dad insisted on attending, I sat in the back with my Nancy Drew mystery, waiting for the magic moment when we would begin to really "do" the convention.

In a mammoth display area, sometimes at hotels as grand as the Waldorf Astoria, I had the chance to fill my shopping bag with all kinds of diminutive items that were becoming staples of camp life in the wake of World War II: picture postcards and paper frames for the annual camp pictures, key rings with camp logos, shiny plastic (known as "gimp") for making lanyards, and nametapes printed in cursive. I was especially taken with the small boxes of Kellogg cereal developed during the war that I could cut, add milk to, and use as a bowl. Most of all, I adored a wood-burning kit that gave off the smell of balsam, to this day my favorite natural perfume.

During the war, there had been no such material splendor, but that was something I failed to realize or appreciate as a girl coming into adolescence so soon after the national emergency. Instead of worrying about collecting ration books from parents, camp directors in the 1950s had to develop written policies to limit the number of supplemental food packages sent by families and friends. And instead of restricting newspapers, camps began to prohibit the use of individual hairdryers and hi-fis as they expanded the cubbies in our cabins or bunks to accommodate the clothing brought by boys as well as girls in excess of the items specified on the printed list, supplied by the camp and pasted inside the top of our regulation metal trunks. In the 1960s, as the traditional camp ethos was challenged by the revolution in sex, drugs, and rock 'n' roll, my father had his first encounters with staff smoking marijuana on night watch and audacious teenagers having sex under an aluminum canoe on the waterfront. In the 1970s, when camps began to specialize in a single sport or activity—sailing or science; more recently computers and weight loss—my father finally put his megaphone and clipboard away, acknowledging that it was a new world, and that the ethos of the campfire and the sing-along had changed forever.

Appendixes

Notes

Sources and Further Reading

Index

Top to bottom: The girls of Camp Cedar hiked to the Blue Mountain Observation Tower around 1920; the boys of Camp Russell learned how to gut fish in 1990; and Unirondack campers enjoyed outdoor activity in the 1990s.

Appendix A

Adirondack Children's Camps, 1885–2005

General note: The information in this list was gleaned from a wide variety of sources, from simple lists in tourist guides to camp brochures and websites. Camp names changed, lake names changed, camps moved, and the records for most are lost. Every attempt has been made to keep this list accurate and comprehensive, and we apologize for any mistakes or omissions.

Note on dates, camp type, and location: Where known, beginning and ending dates of camps are supplied. One date followed by a dash indicates a camp still in operation. "Around" indicates a camp for which a single reference was found; that is, "around 1923" is given for a camp found only in a 1923 guidebook. "Before" and "after" refer to the date of a reference for a camp that was presumably in business before or afterward. "Boys and Girls" denotes a camp having separate campuses with different programs run under the same name and management. Where known, the geographical location is given. This is usually a lake and in the case of lakes with common names, further identification is given. If the lake is not known, a nearby town is given. It is usually the nearest post office as listed in the camp literature.

4-H Camp Overlook

Coed
Indian Lake (Mountain View)
1945–

Operated by Franklin and St. Lawrence County 4-H on the site of the Hotel Overlook. Instructors were initially volunteers and taught first aid and beginning forestry in addition to traditional activities.

4-H Camp Sacandaga

Coed
Sacandaga Lake
1945–2005

4-H purchased the property, which was originally a Civilian Conservation Corps facility, for leadership programs. It was owned and operated by the Fulton/Montgomery, Oneida, and Warren County Cornell Cooperative Extension offices.

Adirondack Camp

Boys (coed after 1979)
Lake George (Glenburnie)
1904–

Dr. Elias G. Brown, formerly the camp doctor at Camp Dudley, founded the camp. It was the official camp of the Buckley School of New York in 1924.

Adirondack Music Camp

Coed
Upper Chateaugay Lake
1934–42

Founder Ralph Hoy felt that "music education could be made an important feature of camp life without sacrificing any of the outdoor sports and camp activities that are so dear to every boy and girl." Closed because of war shortages of staff and food.

Adirondack Scout Reservation

Boys
Piercefield and Long Lake
1990–98

Boy Scout camps operated by the Otetiana and Hiawatha Councils. A total of 5,250 acres in the two locations. After 1999, the two camps were operated separately; see Camp Massawepie and Sabattis Scout Reservation.

Adirondacks Summer Art School

Coed
Unknown
Around 1916

Adirondack Swim Camp

Boys
Lake Lucretia
1944–84

Started by Joe Reiners on the site of Camp Boulder Point. Traditional camp activities were offered in addition to swimming. When Joe Reiners, Jr., took over in the early 1960s, trips became more important and the camp was renamed Adirondack Swim and Trip Camp.

Adirondack Wilderness Camp

Boys
Long Lake
1964–71

On the site of Camp Riverdale. Director Elliott Verner combined an informal camping program with Riverdale traditions. A guiding principle was that boys should compete only with themselves. The land was sold to New York State in 1979 and the buildings taken down in accordance with the "Forever Wild" clause of the state constitution.

Adirondack Woodcraft Camps

Boys (coed after 1989)
Lake Kan-ac-to (Old Forge)
1925–

Founded and directed by William "Chief" Abbott for fifty years. Abbott was a graduate and faculty member of the Syracuse University College of Forestry and also served as Scout Executive with the Boy Scouts. The program has always emphasized an awareness and appreciation of the outdoors, cooperation, and sportsmanship.

Ahmo

Girls
Horseshoe
1922-after 1925

In 1924 the camp promised "with no rigid program to follow, the monotony of the usual camp life is a thing of the past." Progressive education philosophy.

Aldersgate Camp

Coed
Brantingham
1948–

A ministry of the United Methodist Churches of the North Central New York Conference.

Allegro

Unknown
Lake George
Around 1940

ALS-IKH-KAN

Girls
Brantingham Lake
Around 1955
YWCA of Utica

Arcady-In-Pines

Boys
Daisy Lake
Around 1932

Arrowhead Camp

Girls
Lake Champlain
Around 1932

Assisium

Coed
Fourth Lake
Around 1953

Run by Catholic Charities, with seminarians and college students as staff. Religious guidance and instruction were offered; boys only the first four weeks.

Athena

Girls

Lake George (Bolton Landing)

Around 1925

A private estate converted into a camp "for girls of social prominence."

Awanee

Girls

Lake Beebe

Around 1932

Balfour Lake Camp

Boys

Balfour Lake (Minerva)

1919–74

Founded by Sol Amster near Minerva; primarily Jewish campers.

Beaver Camp

Coed

Beaver Lake (Lowville)

Before 1939

The camp was founded by O. T. Anderson and operated as a boys' camp. In 1969 it was purchased by the Adirondack Mennonite Camping Association to provide a Christian camping experience.

Beaver Catholic Boys Camp

Boys

Raquette Lake

1919-after 1931

Big Moose Camp

Boys

Big Moose Lake

1930–48

Owned by the Fort Orange Council Boy Scouts.

The Birches

Girls

Old Forge

Around 1940

Run by the Women's Christian Association of Little Falls, New York.

Black Point

Boys

Ticonderoga

Before 1937-after 1955

Blue Mountain Lodge

Boys

Blue Mountain Lake

Around 1930

Bonheur

Girls

Sacandaga

Around 1939

Boyhaven

Boys

Middle Grove

1932

Schenectady County and Twin Rivers Boy Scout Councils.

Boys' Adirondack Tutorial Camp

Boys

Clintonville

Around 1935

Advertised that boys could "combine vacation with education."

Boys' Club of Utica

Boys

Butler Lake

1953-around 1975

One-week sessions; boys earned the camp fee by selling candy. Operated as a day camp in its last years.

Brant Lake Camp

Boys

Brant Lake

1917–

Founded by Robert Gerstenzang, Joseph Eberly, and John Molloy, three physical education teachers from New York City who had been counselors at Camp Paradox. Clientele mostly Jewish by 1940 when Gerstenzang purchased sole ownership. The camp has always had a strong performing arts component. The first drama counselor was Broadway lyricist Larry Hart. In 1980 added a dance camp for twenty girls aged thirteen to sixteen.

Brownledge

Unknown
Lake Champlain
Around 1940

Brush Hill Camp

Coed
Paul Smiths
1915-after 1926

Run by the principal of the Brush Hill School of Milton, Massachusetts.

Buck Mountain

Boys
Northville
1924-after 1931

Caedmuir Lodge

Boys and Girls
Long Lake
Before 1920-after 1942

Separate campuses; boys under the direction of Bob Beatty and girls under his wife. Each summer the camp held a combined regatta.

Camp "Good Grief"

Coed
Lower St. Regis Lake (Paul Smith's College)
1995

A summer camp program for youth who have experienced the death of a loved one.

Camp Agaming

Boys
Sacandaga Lake (Speculator)
Before 1932–66

Gloversville YMCA. Had a two-week session for girls in August.

Camp Algonquin (1)

Boys (coed after 1946)
Summit Lake
Before 1920–58

A kosher Jewish camp with Friday and Saturday services. Mary Danzinger purchased the camp at a tax sale in 1929 and ran it until 1939 with the help of her daughter and son-in-law, Meyer and Dorothy Schuman. Had an associated guest house, Algonquin Lodge, as well as a resident doctor, nurse, and rabbi.

Camp Algonquin (2)

Boys
Lake George
Around 1932

Camp Anchorage

Boys
Unknown
Around 1938

Camp Arcady

Coed
Lake George (Hague)
1954–70

Louis and Bingo Brandt, owners of the Sagamore Hotel (Bolton Landing), converted the Arcady Country Club to a summer camp for children. The camp provided deluxe accommodations, with fireplaces and private bathrooms in each cottage, steak on Sunday night, a full-time bakery chef, and first-run movies. The clientele was primarily Jewish, but Friday night services were not mandatory.

Camp Arrowhead

Boys
Lake St. Catherine
Around 1932

Camp Askenonta

Coed
Lake Placid (Moose Island)
1949–62

Given to the Onondaga Boy Scout Council by Eugene Schwabach after a fire in which his wife died. In 1955 offered coed camping for Girl Scouts and Campfire Girls; had the first Scout waterskiing program in the country (1952). The property was sold to the State in 1972.

Camp Aweont

Girls
Lake George (Bolton)
1920-after 1924

Later moved and became Carillon.

Camp Baco

Boys
Balfour Lake (Minerva)
1951–

Sol and Cornelia Amster opened Baco as the boys' counterpart to Camp Che-Na-Wah. In 1954 two counselors, Ruth and Melvin Wortman, became partners with the Amsters and then purchased it after Amster's death.

Camp Ballou

Boys
Frankfort Center
1950–

Owned first by Upper Mohawk Boy Scout Council and then by Land of the Oneidas.

Camp Baloo

Girls
Silver Lake
Around 1925

The junior camp of the Silver Lake Camp. Run by the same management.

Camp Beattie

Coed
Long Lake
Around 1953

Camp Bedford

Boys
Clear Pond (Duane)
1946

Owned by Adirondack Council of the Boy Scouts.

Camp Birchwood

Coed
Lake Placid
1948–63

The camp was located on the roadless shore of Lake Placid. Campers could complete a "homesteading" activity, in which they built a lean-to without nails and then slept in it. The property was acquired by New York State in 1963.

Camp Black Elephant

Girls
Lake George (Hulett's Landing)
1910-after 1924

Member of the Woodcraft League.

Camp Boulder Point

Girls
Lake Lucretia
1916-after 1940

Julia Hayes and E. Winnifred Briggs were the directors after 1931, when "the younger girls, and less strong physically, keep busy with handcrafts, plays and operettas, dancing, the editing of the *Log,* and especially nature study." Property purchased in 1944 for the Adirondack Swim Camp.

Camp Bullowa

Boys
Mohegan Lake (Camp Uncas, Raquette Lake)
1972–75

Rockland County Boy Scout Council.

Camp Caravan

Boys
Wheeler Pond
1950-after 1955

Major emphasis on trips. The younger campers went on canoe trips; the oldest campers spent the summer on a western trip covering thirty-four states and seventeen national parks.

Camp Cascade

Boys
Cascade Lake
1938–61

George H. Longstaff (Moss Lake, Cedar Isles, Eagle Cove) purchased the Cascade Lake property during the Depression and opened a camp specializing in riding. Longstaff ceased his involvement during World War II, and the camp had several different owners until the property was purchased by New York State.

Camp Cayuga

Boys
Schroon Lake
1914–70

Jewish.

Camp Cedar Isles

Boys
Fourth Lake
1934–50

George Longstaff (Moss Lake, Camp Cascade, Camp Eagle Cove) purchased the former Cedar Island Camp property—three small islands in Fourth Lake—for a specialty sailing camp.

Camp Cedar

Girls
Pottersville
1908-after 1925

Camp Chateaugay

Coed
Upper Chateaugay Lake
1946–

Lil and Aaron Rose, social workers from Rochester, founded the camp on the site of the Adirondack Music Camp with a Progressive philosophy and the policy of giving 10 percent of the campers full scholarships. In the early years of the camp, these children were refugees from the Holocaust who had been relocated to upstate New York.

Camp Che-Na-Wah

Girls
Balfour Lake
1923–

Sol Amster, a New York City educator who was a codirector of the Balfour Lake Camp, purchased property at the other end of the lake and opened a family camp in 1922. That winter he married Cornelia Schwartz, also an educator, and the following summer they opened the camp as Camp Che-Na-Wah for girls. "Mother Cornel" was a follower of Seton's Woodcraft Indians movement, and Woodcraft rituals were an important part of camp life.

Camp Cherith

Girls
Corinth
1966–

Camp Cherith is a youth ministry of Pioneer Clubs, an evangelical Christian organization.

Camp Cherokee (1)

Coed
Upper Saranac Lake
Before 1955–

Run by Mr. and Mrs. Emmanuel Hirsch of Rochester in the 1950s; in 1963 it was sold to the New York Conference of Seventh Day Adventists.

Camp Cherokee (2)

Boys
Lake Champlain (Willsboro)
Before 1928-after 1932

Camp Chickagami

Boys
Upper Chateaugay Lake
1933–42

Founded by Davis and Adelaide Shoemaker, private schoolteachers, on the site of Camp Miramichi. In addition to standard camp activities, campers learned carpentry, surveying, mapmaking, forestry, boat construction, and motorboat care. When Shoemaker joined the service during World War II, Adelaide ran the camp as a family resort for a few years and then closed it.

Camp Chippewa

Boys
Lake George (Hague)
1916-after 1955

Originally a Catholic camp but nondenominational by 1955. Indian lore, pioneering, and nature study.

Camp Collier

Girls
Raquette Lake
1920-after 1950

In 1920 Anne and Belle Thomson purchased a private camp from the widow of publisher Robert J. Collier. They advertised a "School of Natural Development—a school which stands for advanced and progressive ideals in the science of education."

Camp Crag

Boys
Big Moose Lake
Before 1922– (unknown)

On the site of developer and guide Henry Covey's Camp Crag, built in the 1880s. Founder George Kuhn was a physical education teacher and his wife, Helen, was a music teacher.

Camp De Baun

Boys
Upper Saranac Lake
1966 or earlier–1968

Camp Deborah

Girls
Old Forge
1923-after 1929

Affiliated with Harbor Hill Camp for boys; Jewish.

Camp Deer-Trail

Boys and Girls
Horseshoe Lake
1918-after 1936

Run by Maurice Bernhardt and his family. Primarily Jewish. In 1944 the property became part of the American Legion Mountain Camp for convalescent veterans.

Camp Denton

Boys
Northville
Around 1940

Run by Gloversville Boy Scouts.

Camp Douglas

Boys
Silver Lake
Before 1938-after 1955

Camp Dudley

Boys
Lake Champlain (Westport)
1885–

Founded as a YMCA camp, and now the oldest children's camp in the nation still in operation. Camp tradition includes some Woodcraft League activities (the first council fire was lit by Seton in 1913), and much from the YMCA Christian tradition, such as the camp motto ("The Other Fellow First"), Sunday church service held in the outdoor chapel, Sunday evening hymn sings, and evening Vespers (small group talks on spiritual or moral topics).

Camp Eagle Cove

Boys (coed after 1950)
Fourth Lake (Inlet)
1943–93

Bello Snyder started this camp on the site of Lo-Na-Wo with a predominantly Jewish clientele and the motto "character makes the man."

Camp Eagle Feather

Coed
Raquette Lake
1963–79

Founder Joe Picinich and his wife purchased the former Hunter's Rest hotel as the site for their camp and offered weight lifting and personal defense in addition to traditional activities.

Camp Echo Lake

Coed

Warrensburg

1945–

The camp was founded by New York City educators on the site of a family camp and bungalow colony. Clientele was predominantly Jewish. Since the 1980s the camp has included winter sessions, programs for disadvantaged campers, and trips to the western states.

Camp Fowler

Coed

Sacandaga Lake

1954–

Operated by the Synod of Albany, Reformed Church in America.

Camp Gahada

Boys

1909–about 1917

Stock in camp sold to Schenectady residents, most GE employees. Became a family camp through the 1970s.

Camp Gorham

Coed

Dart's Lake

1961–

Built on the site of Dart's Resort and Boys' Camp. The property was purchased in 1961 by Mr. and Mrs. Jack Gorham and given to the Rochester-area YMCA.

Camp Greylock

Girls

Raquette Lake

1922–71

Founded by the Mason family, who founded Camp Greylock for Boys in the Berkshires. Director Ray Mason, a graduate of Barnard College, was a member of the Child Study Association and had studied with Ernest Thompson Seton. The campers were primarily Jewish. Naomi Levine, owner/director from 1955, believed strongly in preparing girls for a well-rounded life of family, career, and community service.

Camp Guggenheim

Coed

Lower Saranac Lake

1972–

The Roman Catholic Diocese of Ogdensburg's summer resident camp for teens.

Camp Heathcote

Coed

Trout Pond

Around 1953

An interdenominational Christian camp featuring Bible study and chorus.

Camp Hendrick Hudson

Girls

Saranac Lake

Around 1940

Run by the Girl Scouts of Quincy, Massachusetts.

Camp Hoh-Wah-Tah

Girls

Star Lake

1916-after 1925

Camp Horicon

Boys

Brant Lake

1926-unknown

Started by the owners of the Brant Lake Camp for Boys as a men's camp. In 1944 it became the senior division of Brant Lake Camp because of the scarcity of men during World War II.

Camp Idylwold

Boys

Schroon Lake

1916–87

Opened as Idlewood by Oliver Bachrach. Clientele primarily Jewish and from the Baltimore-Washington area and Syracuse. In early years Idylwold had Woodcraft meetings and campfires and was the brother camp for Nawita. In the 1960s the emphasis was changed to sports and the camp claimed to be the first camp in the country to offer tennis as a specialty.

Camp Iroquois

Boys

Lake George (Glen Eyrie)

1900–1918

Established by George F. Tibbitts, YMCA worker and founder of the Gospel Volunteers of the World as part of a family camp that had outgrown its location by 1918 and moved to Speculator. As a family camp it is still in business in Speculator as Camp of the Woods.

Camp Jeanne d'Arc

Girls

Chateaugay Lake

1922–

Founded by Ruth Israel two years after the canonization of Joan of Arc. Israel admired the saint's faith, endurance, courage, and confidence as an example for young women. Predominantly Catholic clientele. From 1927 onward the camp was affiliated with Camp Lafayette for boys, run by Israel's husband, Capt. Charles J. McIntyre.

Camp Kairoa (or Kaiora)

Coed

Upper Chateaugay Lake

1917-after 1941

Frances Sheridan opened her camp as Miss Sheridan's Camp. Soon she was joined by Edna Diggs Gaillard, and they changed the name. Both Sheridan and Gaillard were teachers in private Progressive elementary schools.

Camp Kanuka

Boys

Lake Clear

1916–35

Founded by educators (Peddie School and Bucknell University).

Camp Kingsley

Boys

Bullhead Lake

1921–

Boy Scout camp originally owned by the Rome Council. Currently part of the Revolutionary Trails Council.

Camp Lafayette

Boys

Upper Chateaugay Lake

1927–48

Joseph McIntyre opened Camp Lafayette two years after marrying Ruth Israel, founding director of nearby Camp Jeanne d'Arc. Primarily Catholic campers. Military training and airplane building included.

Camp Lauderdale

Girls

Lake Lauderdale

Before 1934-after 1940

"Sunbaths" one of the activities.

Camp Lavelle

Unknown

Lake Champlain (Cliff Haven)

Around 1939

Camp Lincoln

Boys

Augur Lake

1920–

Founder Colba F. "Chief" Gucker was physical education director at the Lincoln School in New York City. He established a "sister camp," Camp Whippoorwill, in 1931. The two camps are still under family management and have been known since 1947 as North Country Camps.

Camp Lo-Na-Wo

Girls

Fourth Lake

1918-after 1935

The camp name was taken from "Love, Nature, Worth." Jewish clientele and affiliated with Camp Swastika. Girls took a 150-mile canoe trip each summer. The property became Camp Eagle Cove.

Camp MacCready

Girls
Long Pond (Willsboro)
1967–

Established by Sarah and H. Tilden Swan's son Jack, who combined it with Pok-O-Moonshine under one management, calling it Pok-O-MacCready after a great-uncle of Jack Swan and early counselor at Pok-O-Moonshine.

Camp Mark Seven

Coed
Fourth Lake
1981–

Founded by Fr. Thomas Coughlin and the Deaf Catholic Community to offer summer programs for hearing-impaired individuals.

Camp Massawepie

Boys
Massawepie Lake
1920–21

The site of the Hotel Childwold from 1890 to 1909, then the private preserve of the Sykes family, who rented out some of the cottages. Regular renter General Verbeck, headmaster of a military school in Manlius, ran the camp with his son Guido. Boys were taught woodcraft, "orientation" (probably orienteering), and forestry and nature identification, in addition to canoeing and outdoor sports. Tutoring was available for an additional $2/hour.

Camp Mesacosa

Coed
Efner Lake
Around 1910–about 1979

Started by progressive educators and subsequently run for sixty years by Bernardine Yunck and Harriet Brown, the latter director of the Physical Education Department at Skidmore College.

Camp Minnowbrook

Coed
Lake Placid
1949–77

Founders Lothar and Paula Eppstein had emigrated from Germany before the Second World War and established the School for Music Education in New York City in 1941. In 1949 they started The Music Trail, a summer music school in Lake Placid. In 1951 they moved to a former private camp on the roadless side of the lake and expanded to include academic study. By the mid-1960s they not only offered music, drama, and art, but biology, chemistry, rocketry, astronomy, and meteorology.

Camp Miramichi

Girls
Upper Chateaugay Lake
1915–35

Advertised for "girls from Jewish families of culture." Founder Eleanor Deming was a graduate of Bryn Mawr and active in national camping associations, Progressive education, and the Woodcraft League. It also had a small "graduate camp" called Grey Lodge for older girls. Site became Camp Chickagami.

Camp Mohican (1)

Boys
Lake George (Hague)
1909-after 1925

Motto: "Every Camper a Swimmer." Woodcraft activities.

Camp Mohican (2)

Boys
Lake George (Gull Bay)
Around 1953

Operated by the Rye YMCA.

Camp Mondamin

Boys
Schroon Lake
Around 1920

Camp Nahar

Boys
Schroon Lake
Before 1932-after 1939

Jewish.

Camp Naomi

Girls

Schroon Lake

Around 1925

Possibly the "sister camp" to Camp Nahar. Mostly Jewish campers.

Camp Navarac

Girls

Upper Saranac Lake

1952–69

Founder Sara Blum was a prominent Jewish fundraiser who had been a partner in Camp Nawita on Paradox Lake. She purchased the "Great Camp" Prospect Point for a program that prepared girls to realize their full potential in postwar America.

Camp Nawita

Girls

Paradox Lake

1924-after 1952

Jewish. Originally Idylwood was the brother camp under partial same ownership. Closed for a few years during the Depression.

Camp Nay-A-Ti

Girls

Old Forge

Around 1924

Camp Nazareth

Coed

Little Long Lake (Woodgate)

1923–

Operated by Catholic Charities, Diocese of Syracuse.

Camp Niaweh

Girls

Warrensburgh

Before 1941-after 1958

Camp Niqueenum

Girls

Lake Champlain (Willsborough)

1913-after 1923

Probably a summer program of a private school.

Camp Northwood

Coed

Hinckley Reservoir

Before 1950–

Opened on what was then Kuyahoora Lake as a private children's camp operated by Harry and Sylvia Pertz. Closed from the late 1960s until 1976 when it opened as a camp for children with learning disabilities.

Camp of the Seven Pines

Boys

Lake George

1920-after 1924

Predominantly Catholic campers.

Camp Olowan

Unknown

Schroon Lake

Before 1934-after 1941

Camp Onandle

Girls

Chateaugay Lake

Around 1918

Camp Oneida

Boys

Woodgate

1920-after 1936

Nonsectarian, but mostly Jewish. The camp followed the Boy Scout program in 1924.

Camp Onondaga

Boys

Long Lake

Before 1938-after 1968

Cooper French was the director with the longest tenure (ca. 1945–52). He recruited counselors from the Onondaga Reservation near Syracuse. The camp was purchased by National Football League referee Sy Brazy in 1957.

Camp Paradox

Boys

Paradox Lake

1910-after 1965

Started by a former counselor at Schroon Lake Camp who took some Schroon Lake campers and counselors with him when he left. Like Schroon Lake, it was primarily Jewish. Closed in the early 1960s and then reopened for a year or two as a coed camp before closing for good.

Camp Patrick

Boys

Paul Smith's

Around 1941

Run by the Boys' Club of New York City.

Camp Penn

Boys

Lake Champlain (Valcour)

1905-after 1936

Only Christian boys admitted. On arrival boys were divided into small groups, each of which pitched its own tent and constructed its own tent furniture. Field engineering was taught.

Camp Pilgrim

Unknown

Brant Lake

Around 1953

Religious instruction was available.

Camp Pine Log

Girls

Lake Luzerne

1923-after 1970

Founding directors Dorothy Baldwin and Frances Kinnear, graduates of Wellesley College, initially attempted to provide a camp whose price was between that of the organizational camps and the private camps. Costs increased, however, perhaps because they felt that "tennis and golf have become almost required social assets" and had to be taught at camp.

Camp Pocahontas

Girls

Willsboro

1925-after 1929

Near Camp Lincoln. In the late 1920s, this was a sister camp to Camp Lincoln until Lincoln ownership started its own Camp Whippoorwill for girls.

Camp Pok-O-MacCready

See Camp Pok-O-Moonshine.

Camp Pok-O-Moonshine

Boys

Willsboro

1905–

Founded by Charles Alexander Robinson, headmaster of the Peekskill Military Academy. Sports and hiking were emphasized. On his death in 1946 the camp was taken over by his daughter Sarah and her husband, H. Tilden Swan. "Poko" and its associated girls' camp, MacCready, have remained under family ownership as Camp Pok-O-MacCready.

Camp Portaferry

Boys

Lake Portaferry

1947–

Started by the Jefferson-Lewis Boy Scout Council. Now owned by the Hiawatha Seaway Council.

Camp Rainbow

Boys

Schroon Lake

Around 1900

Small camp run by the Junior Branch of the National Sportsman's Association. May not have had a fixed location.

Camp Raquette

Boys

Raquette Lake (Tioga Point)

1952–67

One of four conservation education camps for boys operated by the New York State Department of Conservation. Practical instructional programs included basic wildlife ecology, fly tying, hunter education, and management of woodlots, fisheries, and fur resources.

Camp Red Cloud

Boys
Lake Champlain (Long Point)
1937–69

Founder Louis Lamborn was director of Camp Red Cloud (boys) and Camp Red Wing (girls) in Pennsylvania. In 1936 he moved his camps to the site of Junior Plattsburgh/The Long Point Club/Camp Theodore Roosevelt. Activities included "Wildcraft," which consisted of nature lore, campcraft, Indian lore, and archery. The site is now Point au Roche State Park.

Camp Red Wing (1)

Girls
Schroon Lake
Before 1924-after 1969

Primarily Jewish campers.

Camp Red Wing (2)

Girls
Lake Champlain (Long Point)
1937–69

See Camp Red Cloud.

Camp Regis/Applejack

Coed
Upper St. Regis Lake
1946–

Two camps founded separately by Earl and Pauline Humes: Camp Regis (ages 6–12) and Camp Applejack (ages 13–16). The Humes family's association with the Society of Friends (Quakers) and the Unitarian Universalists influenced a camp philosophy that deemphasized competition and emphasized respect for individuals, particularly those of different backgrounds. On the site of the Gardner-Doing dance camp.

Camp Reliance

Boys
Upper Chateaugay Lake
1916-after 1941

Camp Repton

Boys
Lake Champlain (Port Henry/Keeseville)
1907-after 1932

The Repton School, a private school in Tarrytown, New York, seems to have started summer camps, probably for students at the school, on two occasions. One, started in 1907 by O. C. Roach, was in Port Henry. It was probably closed or moved before 1931, when another Camp Repton shows up in Keeseville.

Camp Restwell

Boys
Lake George (Cleverdale)
1910-after 1941

Camp Resurrection

Coed
Northville
Before 1952-after 1956

Catholic. Operated by the Sisters of the Resurrection, Amsterdam.

Camp Riverdale

Boys
Long Lake
1912–64

Frank Hackett, founder and headmaster of the Riverdale Country School (1907), started the camp so his students could "make a sound and profitable use of the long summer holiday." The program emphasized mountain climbing and canoe trips and followed Ernest Thompson Seton's Woodcraft League model. The campers originally slept in tents but in 1917 Hackett began building permanent structures designed by architect Augustus Shepherd. Hackett died in 1952 and in 1964 the camp was sold and reopened as the Adirondack Wilderness Camp. In 1978 the property was sold to New York State and the buildings were taken down.

Camp Riverside

Boys
Schroon Lake
Before 1915-after 1925

Probably Jewish.

Camp Ronah

Girls

Lake George (Glen Eyrie)

1910-after 1935

Jewish. Run in conjunction with Camp Sagamore for boys. Campers could study French, German, and Italian. Changed ownership and become Wah-Na-Gi some time between 1925 and 1935.

Camp Rondack (1)

Boys

Lower Saranac Lake

Before 1900–1924

Camp Rondack (2)

Girls

Schroon Lake

1920–54

Primarily a Jewish clientele, but considered a nondenominational, secular camp. The property was sold to the Word of Life organization and became their Ranch Camp for teens.

Camp Russell

Boys

White Lake

1918–

The first Boy Scout camp in the Adirondacks. Originally for boys from Utica, Rome, and Herkimer; currently for Herkimer Scouts.

Camp Sagamore

Boys

Lake George (Hague)

1910-after 1941

Affiliated with Wah-Na-Gi (Ronah) for girls. Jewish.

Camp Saskatchewan

Coed

Schroon Lake

1941-after 1956

Previously the Marble Collegiate Camp for girls.

Camp Scenic

Coed

Raquette Lake

Before 1952-after 1955

Located on an island in Raquette Lake.

Camp Severance

Girls

Paradox Lake

1917–72

Predominantly Jewish. Founder "Mother S" (Leopoldine Schwartzkopf) was a teacher, social worker, and clubwoman. A counselor, "Aunt Bunny" (Carrie Sinn), purchased the camp in 1927 and introduced Woodcraft activities. Sabbath services were called "Serious Hour" and tolerance and consideration to others were stressed.

Camp Seyon

Girls

Lake George (Pilot Knob)

Around 1925

A 1924 description of the camp said, "the girls who are unequal to strenuous sports are free to rest and enjoy simple activities, such as sewing, knitting, crocheting and basket making."

Camp Skon-O-Wah

Boys

Chestertown

1926-after 1941

Originally the "younger brother" division of the Mills Adirondack Camp and later run as a separate camp.

Camp So-High

Boys

Raquette River (Long Bow)

Around 1906

Run by the Coit family of Potsdam along with George Brown and Charles Tracy. The emphasis was on woodcraft, canoe trips, and nature study. The directors regarded " 'loafing' as injurious, even in camp life."

Camp Solitude

Coed

Lake Placid

Before 1952-after 1956

A music camp offering private lessons in voice, piano, theory, band, and orchestral instruments as well as traditional activities. Operated by the Kelsall Vocal and Instrumental Studios in Princeton, New Jersey.

Camp Sonrise

Coed

Schroon Lake

1964–

The Missouri Synod of the Lutheran Church purchased the Lakeside Pines property in 1964 and opened a family camp and retreat center with youth programs.

Camp Spruce Ridge

Girls

Old Forge

Before 1955-after 1960

Run by the Syracuse Girl Scout Council as a wilderness advanced campcraft camp. Girls lived in tents and learned canoeing, swimming, and sailing. After passing beginning skills, girls built their own shelters and made a four-to-five-day trip in the High Peaks.

Camp St. Mary

Boys

Long Lake

Before 1947-after 1956

Established on the site of a summer retreat for Catholic seminarians begun in 1915.

Camp Swastika

Boys

Fourth Lake

1920-after 1935

Affiliated with Camp Lo-Na-Wo for girls. Jewish campers and observance of Jewish dietary laws. The camp was closed by the mid-1930s when the name had acquired a more sinister association.

Camp Syracuse

Boys

Seventh Lake

1923–39

A Scout camp affiliated with the Hiawatha Seaway Council. On state land with no permanent structures. Strong forestry component; campers worked on trail construction and fought a forest fire in 1924. First director Fay Welch later founded Tanager Lodge.

Camp Tahawus

Boys

St. Huberts

Around 1925

Woodcraft emphasis.

Camp Tapawingo

Girls

Lake Pleasant

1959–

Established by the Gospel Volunteers, Inc., which also ran neighboring Camp-of-the-Woods, on the only island in Lake Pleasant. "Tapawingo" purportedly means "Place of Joy." Bible study stressed.

Camp Tekakwitha

Boys

Lake Luzerne

1915–76

Run by the Catholic Youth Organization of the Albany diocese and named after The Blessed Kateri Tekakwitha, an Iroquois woman who converted to Catholicism in 1676. Originally located on Brant Lake. Added a girls' program in the interwar years; in the late 1940s moved the girls' program to Pyramid Lake (see Marian Lodge). Later site of the Luzerne Music Center.

Camp Ten-Rab

Girls

Fourth Lake

1922–33

The property was originally a hotel and in its camp days boasted "substantial bungalows," an auditorium, and a bowling alley. Ten-Rab was originally developed by the Bergs as the Jewish girls' camp Cedar Island. George Longstaff purchased it during the Depression and renamed it Cedar Isles.

Camp Timlo

Boys

Lake George (Diamond Point)

1935–75

William G. Morris was the athletic director at the Albany Academy and he initially ran the Timlo property as a summer training camp for his football team.

Camp Treetops

Coed

Lake Placid P.O.

1921–

Founded by Mr. and Mrs. Donald Slesinger, students of John Dewey, with a Progressive philosophy. The camp, which includes a working farm, is currently run by the North Country School, a private middle school.

Camp Triangle

Coed

McCauley Pond

1959–90

Established for mentally retarded youngsters by special education teacher Shirley Schofield on the original site of Camp Apple Jack. Traditional camp activities were adapted for the campers.

Camp Turk

Boys (coed after 1976)

Round Lake (Woodgate)

1924–

Founded as a summer program for the boys and girls, mostly orphans, who were residents of the Masonic Home in Utica in the 1930s and 1940s. Still run by the Masonic Order.

Camp Undercliff

Coed

Lake Placid

Around 1955

Camp Valcour

Boys

Lake Champlain

1919-after 1936

Jewish.

Camp Veritas

Boys

Lake Champlain

Around 1932

Camp Vigor

Boys

Parishville

1922–83

A Boy Scout camp operated by the St. Lawrence County Council; had become "Vigor of the Woods" by the time it closed.

Camp Wabanaki

Girls

Lake George

Around 1910

A 1909 advertisement called it the "most progressive exponent of the camp idea."

Camp Wakonda

Boys (coed after 1955)

Wakonda Lake

Before 1930–1970

Known as "Wakonda-Timberland for Teens" by 1955. In 1971 the property became a camping resort for families in recreational vehicles and tents.

Camp Wakpominee

Boys

Lake George (Log Bay)

1926–

A Boy Scout camp owned by the Mohican Council. Later moved to the town of Lake Luzerne.

Camp Walden

Boys (coed after 1960)

Lake George (Diamond Point)

1938–

Run in the 1930s and 1940s by Charles Garlen, a Glens Falls baker and social activist, for Jewish boys. Had a kosher kitchen and Friday evening Sabbath services.

Camp Walhalla

Boys and Girls

Upper Chateaugay Lake

Before 1903-after 1908

Had two campuses and separate programs. A camp guide took the separate parties fishing and hiking. The boys had a workshop; the girls decorated fungi or made baskets "under the tutelage of an Indian basket maker."

Camp Wanakena

Girls

Lake George

Around 1932

Camp Wego

Boys

Benson

Around 1939

Camp Whippoorwill

Girls

Augur Lake

1931–

Established in 1931 by Colba F. "Chief" Gucker, the founder of nearby Camp Lincoln. Remains in family ownership; see North Country Camps.

Camp Whispering Pines

Girls

South Colton

Unknown

Girl Scout Camp, Thousand Islands Council.

Camp Windymere

Boys

Blue Mountain Lake

Before 1912-after 1918

Director George Ottaway was an Episcopal priest and the camp was located at his island camp. Tutoring was available. "Everything was in true wilderness style, except the table, which was generously supplied with the best the markets afford."

Camp Winnakee

Girls

Lake Placid

1922-after 1925

Run by Katharine Quinn and Anna Mohair, both of whom were graduates of Columbia University and high school teachers in Newark, New Jersey.

Camp Winona

Girls

Schroon Lake

Around 1920

Camp Woodmere

Girls

Paradox Lake

1916–89

Primarily Jewish clientele; "short, impressive religious services" were held each Saturday morning in the 1940s.

Camp Woodsmoke

Girls (later coed)

Lake Placid

1964–

As printed in a brochure during the early years, "An original, free-form approach to leadership growth and self-discovery in the teen years."

Carillon

Girls

Ticonderoga

1923-after 1941

Begun by Mae Nally, formerly codirector of Aweont.

Cedar Island Camp

Girls

Fourth Lake

1916–

Jewish. Mrs. Ray Phillips started the camp on Fourth Lake. In the early 1920s she purchased the Antlers Hotel on Raquette Lake (see Raquette Lake Girls Camp) and moved the younger girls there. After about 1925 she sold Cedar Island (see Ten-Rab).

Cedar Lodge

Boys

Silver Lake

1942–65

Founder Francis B. Sprague was an educator in the northeastern Adirondacks. Most of the counselors at Cedar Lodge were fellow teachers, and the campers came from the same area or from the Albany area. In the 1950s the Sprague family changed the camp from a boys' camp to a family camp.

Cedarlands

Boys

Lake McRorie (Long Lake)

1963–

The property was originally a private camp, which was sold to the Upper Mohawk Council Boy Scouts. With 5,500 acres, it is the largest Scout camp in the Adirondacks. Includes a forty-foot climbing and rappelling tower. Now owned by the Revolutionary Trails Council.

Champlain

Coed

Lake Champlain (Westport)

Before 1950-after 1960

Roller skating was on the program.

Chateaugay Camp Lodge

Boys

Upper Chateaugay Lake

Around 1923

Opened in 1923 as a "high class" boys' summer school on the grounds of Sunset Inn. A Middlebury College professor was director.

Chepontuc

Girls

Palmer Pond

1935–43

Run by the Adirondack Council of Girl Scouts. There was no phone; a neighbor boy was sent with messages and equipped with a whistle he would blow to warn any skinny-dippers of his approach.

Chimney Mountain Reservation

Boys

Indian Lake (?)

1976

Boy Scout camp, Southern New Jersey Council.

Chingachgook

Boys (coed after 1975)

Lake George (Pilot Knob)

1913–

Originally run by the Schenectady YMCA; now the Capital District Y.

Cliff Haven

Boys

Lake Champlain

1897-after 1932

Part of the Catholic Summer School of America, a chautauqua-like institution south of Plattsburgh that catered to Catholic families. In the early years the counselors were seminarians and the boys used some of the facilities of the summer school. By the 1930s the camp had all its own facilities and the counselors were mostly "college men."

Corsican

Boys

Lake George (Diamond Point)

Around 1926

The camp was on the site of the Corsican School, a boarding school about which little is known. The director/headmaster, J. Howard Randerson, called himself Prince Napoleon Bonaparte V. No smoking or profanity was allowed.

Crescent Bay

Unknown

Lower Saranac Lake

Before 1934-after 1940

Crooning Pines

Unknown

Warrensburg

Around 1940

Crown Point

Boys

Lake Champlain (Crown Point)

1921–35

Curtis S. Read Scout Reservation

Boys

Brant Lake

1951–

Scout reservation operating three smaller camps: Camp Waubeeka (patrol cooking camp), Camp Buckskin (dining hall camp), and Summit Base (high adventure base). Founded by the Fenimore Council; currently run by the Westchester-Putnam Council.

Dart's Camp

Boys

Dart's Lake

1927–38

Run as part of a hunting lodge and resort by the resort owners and a professor from Columbia so that campers could stay near their parents for the summer. The 1930 camp brochure promised reinforcement of the values of frankness, honesty, fair play, and "helpful manliness." In 1962 the site became YMCA Camp Gorham.

Dart's Camp for Girls

Girls

Dart's Lake

Around 1930

A short-lived girls' session at Dart's Camp.

Deep Woods

Girls

Chilson

Around 1940

Run by Albany Girl Scouts.

Deer Head

Coed

Elizabethtown

Around 1923

Deerfoot Lodge

Boys

Whitaker Lake

1930–

YMCA worker Alfred Kunz started Deerfoot Lodge with the aim of providing a camp for boys in "their difficult adolescent years." "Pop" Tibbitts, director of nearby Camp of the Woods, helped him establish a camp to provide "sane, constructive religious teaching of a solidly biblical nature." The camp briefly had a girls' session (Kariwiyo Lodge).

Deerhurst

Unknown

Thendara

Around 1939

Deerwood Adirondack Music Center

Coed

Upper Saranac Lake

1943–57

Sherwood Kains (formerly of Adirondack Music Camp) started Deerwood with the financial backing of some Saranac Lake businessmen. Kains's connections in the musical world resulted in a distinguished faculty that included Béla Bartók in 1944. Campers gave concerts at least once a week.

Double H-Hole in the Woods Camp

Coed

Lake Vanare

1992–

Charles R. Wood, owner and developer of The Great Escape amusement park, founded the camp in partnership with actor Paul Newman. "Double H" stands for "health and happiness." The camp serves children with physical and emotional challenges who would not be able to attend traditional camps.

East Caroga Lake

Girls

East Caroga Lake

Around 1940

Run by the Gloversville YWCA.

Echo Camp

Girls
Raquette Lake
1946–87

A high-end camp founded and run for thirty-five years by Frances Clough on the site of a "Great Camp" accessible only by water. Campers lived in the rustic cabins built in the 1880s and traveled to church and town in the camp's thirty-foot 1927 launch. Strong emphasis on aquatic skills.

Forest Lake Camp

Boys and Girls
Warrensburg
1926–

Established by Harold Confer and continues in family management.

Forestcraft

Boys (coed after 1977)
Upper Saranac Lake
1948–

Dr. Ted Blackmar, school physician at Lawrenceville and Peddie schools, founded the camp primarily to provide backcountry trips in small groups. Largest number of campers in one year was twenty-five. Trips include the White Mountains in New Hampshire and Mt. Kahtadin in Maine as well as Adirondacks.

Fox Lair

Boys
Baker's Mills
Before 1939–54

In a former private camp, open to members of the Police Athletic League boys' club.

French Recreation Class for Girls

Girls
Lake Placid
Around 1896

Probably the first exclusively girls' camp in the country. Facilities included a piano, and activities included study of French, boating, and tramping. A.k.a. French Vacation Class for Girls.

Ga-He-Ge

Boys
Old Forge
1921-after 1932

Gardner-Doing

Coed
Upper St. Regis Lake
1916-after 1936

Ruth Gardner and Gail Doing, members of the New York City Ballet, purchased the private camp of the Penfold family on Upper St. Regis Lake for their camp. Campers learned the Ruth Doing System of Rhythmics. Doing probably also ran the eponymous music camp.

Gibbons

Boys
Horicon
1931-after 1941

Run by the Catholic Diocese of Albany. Seems to have moved to Brant Lake by 1939.

Girl Scout Camp Eagle Island

Girls
Upper Saranac Lake
1938–

Run by the Girl Scout Council of Greater Essex and Hudson County (New Jersey). Uses a camp designed by Saranac Lake architect William Coulter for U.S. vice president and New York State governor Levi P. Morton.

Grachusut

Boys
White Lake
Around 1953

Operated by Grace Church, Utica, and open only the last week in August to boys of the congregation.

Green Mountain

Boys
Lake Hortonia
Around 1932

Half Moon

Boys
Keeseville
Around 1939

Harbor Hill

Boys
Old Forge
1923-after 1929

Affiliated with Camp Deborah for girls. Jewish.

Hawkeye Trail Camps

Boys and Girls
Silver Lake
1926–78

The camp was started in Maine in 1913 and then moved to the site of the former Camp Baloo. Helen Post Hartz ("Hartzie") ran the camp from at least 1939 until her death in 1978. In 1926 the boys' section was called Whipowill, the girls' section Kokosing, and there was an associated club for parents and other adults.

Hawkeye

Boys
Adirondack
Around 1935

Herkimer County YMCA Camp

Coed
Fourth Lake
Date unknown

Hidden Lake Girl Scout Camp

Girls
Lake George
1938–

Founded by the Schenectady Girl Scouts. Currently run by the Mohawk Pathways Council.

High Peaks Camp for Boys

Boys
Upper Ausable Lake
Around 1967

Run for the Adirondack Trail Improvement Society (ATIS) by two private-school teachers and one of their wives.

Hitchins Park Camp

Boys
Bog River
1976–81

Boy Scout Camp, Suffolk County Council.

In-Ca-Pah-Cho

Girls
Long Lake
1929-after 1936

Junior Plattsburgh

Boys
Lake Champlain (Long Point)
1917–24

A precursor of the Reserve Officer Training Corps, the Plattsburgh training camp provided military training for young men. In 1924 the camp changed hands and became the Long Point Club, then Camp Theodore Roosevelt, and ultimately Camp Red Cloud.

Kamp Kamargo

Boys
Lake Bonaparte
1921–46

Boy Scout Camp, Jefferson-Lewis Councils.

Kariwiyo Lodge

Girls
Whitaker Lake
1937–42

The idea of "Mom" Kunz, wife of the founder of Deerfoot Lodge. It operated for two years in rented facilities in the hamlet of Sabael on Indian Lake. It then moved to Deerfoot, where it ran the last two weeks of the summer season. In the 1940s Deerfoot's boys' programs took precedence. "Kariwiyo" was supposedly the Iroquois word for "good news."

Kee-Yo-No

Boys
Old Forge
1920-after 1940

Jewish clientele.

Kempchel

Boys
Long Lake
Around 1925

Kent Camp

Boys
Warm Pond
1912–20

A project of the private Kent School, which was founded in 1906. Located on property owned by the well-known conservationist John Bird Burnham. Tutoring was provided for boys who were falling behind in their studies or who were preparing for advanced courses. The camp provided "every kind of out-door amusement" for all. After the camp closed the site was rented by Camp Lincoln.

Kinikinick

Girls
Lake St. Catherine
Around 1932

Kowaunkami

Girls
Caroga Lake
Before 1952-after 1970

Run by the Fulton County Girl Scouts.

Kun-Ja-Muk

Boys
Speculator
1920-after 1941

Kuyrahoora Children's Camp

Coed
Lake Kuyrahoora
Around 1936

La Jeunesse

Boys
First Fish Creek Pond
1916–56

Founded and run for almost forty years by "Hank" Blagden, whose family had a camp in the area. Included military training during World War I. The camp grew rapidly and had many campers from prominent New York families who contributed generously to camp improvements, including an infirmary called the Ritz because it was the only place in camp where boys could sleep in a bed and have a hot bath.

Lake Clear Camp

Girls
Lake Clear
Around 1970

Owned by the North Country Girl Scout Council.

Lake Colby

Boys (coed after 1971)
Lake Colby
1967–

Operated by the New York State Department of Environmental Conservation (DEC) for New York State residents on the site of a former private camp. Initially focused on wildlife management, but in the 1970s the program changed to encompass many aspects of environmental management. Lake Colby was the first DEC camp to admit girls.

Lake George Camp for Girls

Girls
Lake George
1955-after 1958

Taught square dancing as well as traditional camp activities.

Lake George Camp

Boys
Lake George (Hague)
1923-after 1940

In the 1930s the camp was run by Major Allan Smith and "a militaristic atmosphere prevails."

Lake Placid Camp

Boys
Lake Placid
1918-after 1925

French lessons were available.

Lake Placid Soccer Camp

Coed
Lake Placid
1976–

One of the few specialty sports camps in the Adirondack region.

Lakeside Pines

Girls

Schroon Lake

1946–63

Stressed "the sociable sports," golf and tennis. Cabins were outfitted like private homes. Primarily Jewish campers, most from Montreal. The first counselors were graduates of Columbia Teachers College. Property sold to the Missouri Synod of the Lutheran Church (see Camp Sonrise).

Log Cabin

Girls

Unknown

1926-after 1941

Lone Pine

Boys

Osgood Lake

1921-after 1956

In addition to overnight trips at "rough camp," the boys made Pathé motion pictures and had a ninety-minute study period each day.

Long Lake Camp for the Arts

Coed

Long Lake

1969–

David Katz, the director of the Queens Symphony Orchestra, and his wife purchased the Stonegate Music and Arts Camp to open their own camp focused on the creative arts. The first year it was called the Long Lake Creative Arts and Work Camp and later became Long Lake Creative Arts Camp. Traditional camp activities are combined with arts and crafts, dance, drama, music, radio/TV/video, and circus, culminating in performances.

Long Point Club

Boys

Lake Champlain

1919–23

On the site of Junior Plattsburgh. Activities included football, baseball, tennis, basketball, track and field, golf, and even polo. Tutoring was under the auspices of the Roxbury School. The club reported six hundred campers one season, unusually large for a children's camp. Became Camp Theodore Roosevelt.

Luzerne Music Center

Coed

Lake Luzerne

1980–

Bert Phillips founded the camp on the site of the former Camp Tekakwitha. Features chamber and large ensemble experience, faculty recitals, trips to the ballet in Saratoga, and private instruction in instrumental and vocal music and conducting.

Lynx Camp

Boys

Raquette Lake

1949–78

Early motto was "An informal education for the sportsman's son." Started by George Linck, a physical education instructor at West Point, with George Fuge on Sacandaga Lake. In 1966 the camp moved to Big Island in Raquette Lake. Primarily a tripping camp, with progressively longer trips as campers got older. In 1974 a three-week session was offered for girls. The counselors were mostly the Linck sons, of whom there were six.

Ma-Ho-Ge

Coed

Swan Lake

1927-after 1935

Jewish.

Manhattan Camp

Boys

Schroon Lake

1917-after 1933

Catholic.

Maple-Wold

Boys

St. Regis Lake

Around 1909

Advertised as "for School and College Boys"; possibly a tutorial camp.

Marble Collegiate Camp

Girls

Schroon Lake

Around 1940

Run by the Marble Collegiate Church of New York City. Later Camp Saskatchewan.

Marian Lodge

Girls

Paradox Lake

1946–72

Albany's Bishop Gibbons purchased the former Pyramid Club property to establish a camp for working-and middle-class Catholic girls. Originally campers came for just one week. By the late 1950s longer programs were offered. When closed by the diocese a former staff member opened it as the Pyramid Life Camp for seminars and retreats.

Massawepie Scout Camps

Boys

Massawepie Lake

1952–

Consisted of four different camps over time: Camp Pioneer (1952–70 and 1977), Camp Mountaineer (1953–1999), and Camp Voyageur (1958–1976), all located on Massawepie Lake. Camp Forester, a specialized patrol-cooking camp on Deer Pond, ran from 1969 to 1994. Camp Pioneer was renovated and reopened in 2000, and is the current Scout summer camp. The separate Adirondack Trek program for older Scouts and Venturers is also based at Massawepie.

Meadowmount School of Music

Coed

Westport

1944–

A summer school for accomplished young string players training for professional careers in music. Alumni include Itzhak Perlman and Yo-Yo-Ma. Founded on the site of a private estate by Ivan Galamian, then regarded as the world's leading violin teacher. Since 1954 run by the Society for Strings, Inc.

Meenahga Lodge

Boys

Rainbow Lake (Onchiota)

1903-after 1975

Originally developed as a summer program of the Adirondack-Florida School, now Ransom Everglades School. The school sold the camp in 1946. Under new ownership Camp Meenahga focused on aquatics. By 1953 Buster Crabbe, actor and two-time Olympic freestyle medalist, was involved. In the 1970s Arthur Sherman was director, providing kosher food and all sorts of aquatic activities including scuba.

Mills Adirondack Camp and Summer School of Classic Dancing

Girls

Chestertown

1922-after 1940

A visitor in 1928 reported "an exhibition of folk and classic dancing and some extraordinary recitations, songs and acting by talented youngsters." The young brother division of this camp later became Skon-O-Wah.

Moon Hill

Unknown

Schroon Lake

Before 1950-after 1956

Word of Life now owns the Moon Hill property.

Moose River Baptist Youth Camp

Coed

Lyonsdale

Around 1970–

Moss Lake Camp

Girls

Moss Lake

1923–72

George Longstaff's most successful camp project. Lifelong skills such as fencing, horseback riding, dramatics, riflery, bridge, typing, painting, and classical ballet were taught in addition to traditional camp activities. "The Camp of Experts" had among its aims developing "socially well-equipped young ladies."

Moss Lodge

Girls

Lake George

Before 1974–79

Taken over by Adirondack Camp for Boys in 1975 but still run separately; in 1979 merged to form the coed Adirondack Camp.

New York State Music Camp

Coed
Otter Lake
1947–55

Started by Dr. Frederick Swift to provide advanced music education for high school students. Operated in the former Otter Lake Hotel. The camp outgrew the facility and moved to Oneonta. Band, orchestra, choir, radio, and baton twirling as well as traditional camp activities.

Nokomis Lodge

Boys
Rainbow Lake
Around 1913

Codirectors were public-school teachers in Dunkirk, New York. Forestry and woodcraft were taught as well as traditional camp activities.

Normandie

Coed
Lake Champlain (Westport)
1972–

A traditional children's camp founded in New Hampshire in 1966 offering French language instruction. Moved to the Adirondacks, and in the 1980s the program was revised to specialize in water sports including windsurfing, scuba, and personal watercraft.

North Country Camps

See Camp Lincoln, Camp Whippoorwill

North Star Camps

Boys and Girls
Duane
1945–62

Orthodox Jewish with a kosher kitchen and two Sabbath services each week. In 1953 the camp advertised a "traditional Jewish religious program." In the early 1960s it was run by Ben Sacks of Brooklyn and called Star Lake. The campers were primarily from Montreal and New York City.

Northern Frontier Camp

Boys
North River
1946–

Run by the Christian Service Brigade.

Nun-Da-Sah

Boys
Thendara
1925-after 1936

Old Furnace Point

Coed
Lake Champlain
Around 1953

Osgood

Unknown
Paul Smith's
Unknown

Oswegatchie Camp

Coed
Croghan
1946–

Operated by the New York Future Farmers Leadership Training Foundation. Currently operated as a youth camp during the summer months and as an educational, recreational retreat center the remainder of the year.

Our Lady of Fatima

Girls
Lake Champlain
Around 1952

This girls' camp was operated on the grounds of the Catholic Summer School at Cliff Haven by the Grey Nuns of the Sacred Heart, Philadelphia.

Outlet

Boys
Old Forge
Before 1934-after 1941

Another of George Longstaff's ventures.

Owaissa

Girls
Indian Lake
1917-after 1941

Deer jacking (presumably with a light only as this method of hunting was illegal) was "a feature of camp life" in 1925.

Owlyout

Girls

Upper Chateaugay Lake

Around 1932

Pack Forest

Coed

Warrensburgh

1998–

The most recent New York State Department of Environmental Conservation camp. Offering a high school-level program in environmental studies.

Peniel Bible Youth Camp

Coed

Lake Luzerne

Before 1930–

An interdenominational religious camp founded by the Methodist and the Calvary Orthodox Presbyterian Churches in Schenectady for the city's youth on the site of Song-Hawk.

Pine Camp

Boys

Harkness

1923-after 1929

Pine Tree Camp

Boys

Schroon Lake

Before 1917-after 1932

Mostly Jewish.

Pinewood School

Unknown

Keene Valley

1952-after 1955

A reading and study skills summer program of the Pinewood School of Summerville, South Carolina, to help meet the "increasing demands for higher standards in education."

Piseco Lake

Boys

Piseco Lake

1961–62

Boy Scout camp.

Point O'Pines Camp

Girls

Brant Lake

1957–

The property was initially developed as a family resort by the owners of the Brant Lake Camp. One of the few remaining private girls' camps in the region.

The Ranch

Girls

Lake Clear

1989–

A specialty horseback riding camp. Overnight pack trips, roundups, trail rides, rodeos, dressage, cross country, and jumping.

Raquette Lake Boys' Camp

Boys

Raquette Lake

1922–

Primarily Jewish initially. Also known as Raquette Lake Boys' Club. Founded by Mrs. Ray Phillips on Woods Point in Raquette Lake when she moved her Cedar Island girls' camp to the region in the early 1920s. Partners Mr. and Mrs. Max Berg were first directors, followed by Raymond Riordan, an educator who ran his own private school near New York City and, briefly, the Wilderness Camp in the Adirondacks. In 1951 the boys' and girls' camps were sold to separate owners. They were reunited under the same management in 1973.

Raquette Lake Camps

Boys and Girls

Raquette Lake

1916–

See Raquette Lake Boys' Camp and Raquette Lake Girls' Camp.

Raquette Lake Girls' Camp

Girls

Raquette Lake

1916–

Jewish; also known as "Club." Began as an offshoot of the Cedar Island Camp. About 1922 director Ray Phillips purchased the Antlers Hotel property on Raquette Lake for her camp, housing the girls in tents on the grounds. A visitor wrote that the camp "occupies the estate of a former hotel, with lovely Casino and lodges and lean-tos and lawns, the most picturesque dining-hall I have ever seen, and its own gardens and stables and steam-laundry." Phillips also started Raquette Lake Boys' Camp.

Rollins Pond Adventure Base

Boys

Rollins Pond

1965–

A wilderness Scout camp that is part of Northern New Jersey Council. When the camp was first opened, "wilderness camping" was a relatively new idea. The camp moved to its present site on West Pine Pond in 1970.

Rondax

Boys (then coed)

Rondaxe Lake

1921-after 1955

Jewish. The camp opened and closed several times, changing its name slightly each time. Was known variously as Camp Rondax, Rondax Club, Rondaxe Lake Camp.

Ronwood

Boys

Warren County

Around 1969

Rotary

Boys

Lake George

Around 1940

Run by the Schenectady Boy Scouts.

Ruth Doing Music Camp

Unknown

Chateaugay Lake

Around 1925

Ruth Doing also codirected the Gardner-Doing Camp.

Sabattis Adventure Camp

Boys

Long Lake

1959–

Scout camp on the former Goodyear estate. Some of the estate buildings and a cleared area once used as a nine-hole golf course are used by the Scouts. Owned by Patriot's Path Council of New Jersey.

Sabattis Scout Reservation

Boys

Lows Lake

1958–

A traditional full-featured patrol cooking camp considered the premier wilderness Scout camp in the Northeast. The property was developed by A. A. Low around 1900 as a commercial enterprise producing timber, maple syrup and candy, wine, and preserves. With Camp Portaferry and Trek Camp (based at Sabattis), comprises The Adirondack Scout Camps, owned by the Hiawatha Seaway Council.

Sacandaga Bible Conference

Coed

Broadalbin

1969–

Evangelical Christian program.

Sagamore Reading Camp

Coed

Sagamore Lake

Around 1960

Probably run by the University College of Syracuse University. Program included note-taking, written and oral expression, study skills, poetry appreciation, fiction evaluation, and research paper writing. Housed in the Durant-designed Camp Sagamore.

Salvation Army Camp

Unknown

Saddle Lake

Around 1969

Sans Souci

Boys

Lake Pleasant

Around 1950

Boy Scout Camp run by the Twin Rivers Boy Scout Council.

Schroon Lake Camp

Boys

Schroon Lake

1906–60

Founder Isaac Moses was a prominent Reform Jewish rabbi in Manhattan. The first campers were children of his congregation. Property became part of Word of Life.

Schroon Lodge

Boys

Schroon Lake

Before 1952-after 1956

Schroon Nahar

Boys

Schroon Lake

Around 1925

Silver Bay Travel Camp

Boys

Lake George (Silver Bay)

Around 1935

Silver Lake Camp

Girls

Silver Lake

1911–72

Founder Nina Hart, principal of a private girls' school, ran the camp until 1945, when she sold it to three counselors, Betty Hicks, Hazel Kinsley, and Gladys Pazel. Girls slept on sleeping porches of a lodge designed for the camp. Camp Baloo was the junior camp.

Skye Farm Camp

Coed

Lake George (Bolton Landing)

1969–

Operated by Troy Annual Conference of the United Methodist Church, Camping and Retreat Ministries.

Snowy Mountain Camp

Boys

Indian Lake (Sabael)

1930-after 1936

A Woodcraft camp.

Somerhill

Coed

Athol

Before 1968-after 1980

Campers were mostly from New York City. The camp had a riding and horse care program and an Olympic-sized pool.

Song-Hawk

Boys

Lake Luzerne

1930–37

A Woodcraft camp. Site became Peniel Bible Youth Camp.

Southwoods

Coed

Paradox Lake

1998–

On the site of Camp Woodmere.

Spruce Mountain

Boys and Girls

Warrensburg

Before 1934-after 1941

The directors also ran a two-week winter camp in Florida.

St. Bernard's Summer Camp

Boys

St. Regis Falls

1919-after 1939

Affiliated with St. Bernard's School for boys, New York. An hour each day devoted to study. A.k.a. Camp St. Bernard.

St. George Pathfinder's Camp

Coed

Great Sacandaga Lake

1966–

Russian exiles brought many traditions with them to the United States, including scouting. The Russian scouting program, which has remained distinct from the Boy Scouts of America, includes scouting songs in Russian, campfires, camping out, and waterfront activities.

Star Lake

See North Star Camps

Stonegate Music and Arts Camp

Coed
Long Lake
1964–65
Stonegate occupied the site of Stonegate Lodge, a resort on Long Lake that had been a private camp. The site is now occupied by the Long Lake Camp for the Arts.

Taft

Boys
Lake Clear
1912-after 1941
Primarily a tutoring camp.

Tanager Lodge

Coed
Upper Chateaugay Lake
1925–
Founder Fay Welch, a naturalist and musician, was a personal friend of Ernest Thompson Seton and his camp program was modeled after the Woodcraft program. Camp has changed little since then either in the activities, the housing (platform tents), or the philosophy.

Thatcher Outpost Camp

Boys
Raquette Lake
1976–90
Boy Scout Camp, Governor Clinton and Twin Rivers Councils.

Theodore Roosevelt Camp for Boys

Boys
Lake Champlain (Long Point)
1924–34
Situated on the site of the former Junior Plattsburgh Training Camp, which afterwards operated briefly as the Long Point Club. Later became Red Wing (2) and Red Cloud.

Ticonderoga

Boys and Girls
Ticonderoga
1916-after 1956

Timberland

Unknown
Schroon Lake
Around 1963
By 1966 the camp property had become part of the Word of Life camp.

Totem Camp

Coed
Harrisville
1938-after 1956
Director Bill Graf was the athletic director and coach at Watertown High School. The camp, a former private estate, was located on the Oswegatchie River. Most of the campers came from Watertown and Gouverneur. State University of New York-Brockport purchased the property, after which the Fulton school district ran a summer school there for several years.

Trout Lake Camp

Girls
Lake George (Bolton)
Around 1925

Twin Lakes

Boys
Whitehall
Around 1932

Twin Rocks

Coed
Lake Champlain
Around 1953
Had a western flavor with overnight covered-wagon trips, square dances, and riding.

Unirondack

Coed
Beaver Lake (Lowville)
1951–
A Unitarian Universalist Camp and Retreat Center.

Wah-Na-Gi

Girls
Lake George (Glen Eyrie)
1914-after 1936
Jewish. Formerly Ronah.

Wah-Pe-Ton

Boys
Ticonderoga
Around 1940

Warren County Children's Health Camp

Coed
Warrensburg
1922-after 1968

Initially run by the Warren County Tuberculosis Commission for children either from tuberculosis families or malnourished children needing training in good health habits. From 1923 to the 1950s parent instruction classes were given. Girls came in July; boys came in August. By 1967 it was run by the Warren County Health Association.

Wa-Tah-Wah

Girls
Lake George (Bolton)
Around 1923

Affiliated with the Adirondack Girl Scout Council serving Girl Scouts from Glens Falls, Fort Ann, Corinth, Ticonderoga, and Bolton Landing.

White Lake Camp

Unknown
White Lake
Around 1969

Run by the Episcopal Diocese of Albany.

Wilderness Camp

Boys
Bog River (Horseshoe)
Before 1920-after 1925

The camp was run by Raymond Riordan of the Raymond Riordan School at Highland in Ulster County. Horseshoe was the community on the Bog River established by Augustus A. Low for loggers and other workers on his estate.

Willow Hill Farm

Coed
Keeseville
1980s–

Specialty horseback riding camp.

Woodworth Lake Scout Reservation

Boys
Woodworth Lake
1949–

Boy Scout camp affiliated with the Twin Rivers Boy Scout Council.

Word of Life

Coed
Schroon Lake
1946–

Word of Life Fellowship, Inc., a fundamental, evangelical organization founded in 1942, purchased the former Clark estate on an island in Schroon Lake in 1946 to open a camp for teens. In 1955 they added a dude ranch camp for younger children. In the early twenty-first century their youth divisions, The Rock and The Ranch, each hosted 3,200–4,000 children per summer.

Wurths'

Boys
Schroon Lake
Around 1955

Young Life Saranac Village

Coed
Upper Saranac Lake
1969–

Young Life, an evangelical, fundamentalist Christian organization dedicated to youth ministry, was founded in 1941. The organization operates youth camps all over the country. Saranac Village is on the site of Camp Navarac, itself formerly the estate of Adolph Lewisohn.

Appendix B

Adirondack Children's Camps by Location

Adirondack

Hawkeye

Athol

Somerhill

Augur Lake

Camp Lincoln
Camp Whippoorwill

Baker's Mills

Fox Lair

Balfour Lake (Minerva)

Balfour Lake Camp
Camp Baco
Camp Che-Na-Wah

Beaver Lake (Lowville)

Beaver Camp
Unirondack

Benson

Camp Wego

Big Moose Lake

Big Moose Camp
Camp Crag

Bog River

Hitchins Park Camp
Wilderness Camp

Bolton Landing

Skye Farm Camp

Blue Mountain Lake

Blue Mountain Lodge
Camp Windymere

Brant Lake

Brant Lake Camp
Camp Horicon
Camp Pilgrim
Curtis S. Read Scout Reservation
Point O'Pines Camp

Brantingham

Aldersgate Camp

Brantingham Lake

ALS-IKH-KAN

Broadalbin

Sacandaga Bible Conference

Bullhead Lake

Camp Kingsley

Butler Lake

Boys' Club of Utica

Caroga Lake

Kowaunkami

Cascade Lake

Camp Cascade

Chateaugay Lakes

Camp Onandle
Ruth Doing Music Camp

Chestertown

Camp Skon-O-Wah
Mills Adirondack Camp and Summer
    School of Classic Dancing

Chilson

Deep Woods

Clear Pond (Duane)

Camp Bedford

Clintonville

Boys' Adirondack Tutorial Camp

Corinth

Camp Cherith

Croghan

Oswegatchie Camp

Daisy Lake

Arcady-In-Pines

Dart's Lake

Dart's Camp

Dart's Camp for Girls

Camp Gorham

Duane

North Star Camps

East Caroga Lake

East Caroga Lake

Elizabethtown

Deer Head

Fish Creek Ponds

La Jeunesse

Fourth Lake

Assisium

Camp Cedar Isles

Camp Eagle Cove

Camp Lo-Na-Wo

Camp Mark Seven

Camp Swastika

Camp Ten-Rab

Cedar Island Camp

Herkimer County YMCA Camp

Frankfort Center

Camp Ballou

Great Sacandaga Lake

St. George Pathfinder's Camp

Harrisville

Totem Camp

Harkness

Pine Camp

Hinckley Reservoir

Camp Northwood

Horicon

Gibbons

Horseshoe Lake

Ahmo

Camp Deer-Trail

Indian Lake (Franklin County)

4-H Camp Overlook

Indian Lake (Hamilton County)

(?) Chimney Mountain Reservation

Owaissa

Snowy Mountain Camp

Keene Valley

Pinewood School

Keeseville

Half Moon

Willow Hill Farm

Lake Beebe

Awanee

Lake Bonaparte

Kamp Kamargo

Lake Champlain

Arrowhead Camp

Brownledge

Camp Cherokee (Willsboro)

Camp Dudley (Westport)

Camp Lavelle (Cliff Haven)

Camp Niqueenum (Willsborough)

Camp Penn (Valcour)

Camp Red Cloud (Long Point)

Camp Red Wing (Long Point)

Camp Repton

Camp Valcour

Camp Veritas

Champlain (Westport)

Cliff Haven

Crown Point

Junior Plattsburgh

Long Point Club

Normandie (Westport)

Old Furnace Point

Our Lady of Fatima

Theodore Roosevelt Camp for Boys (Long Point)

Twin Rocks

Lake Clear

Camp Kanuka

Lake Clear Camp

Taft

The Ranch

Lake Colby

Lake Colby

Lake George

Adirondack Camp (Glenburnie)

Allegro

Athena (Bolton Landing)

Camp Algonquin

Camp Arcady (Hague)

Camp Aweont (Bolton)

Camp Black Elephant (Hulett's Landing)

Camp Chippewa (Hague)

Camp Iroquois (Glen Eyrie)

Camp Mohican (Gull Bay & Hague)

Camp of the Seven Pines

Camp Restwell (Cleverdale)

Camp Ronah (Glen Eyrie)

Camp Sagamore (Hague)

Camp Seyon (Pilot Knob)

Camp Timlo (Diamond Point)

Camp Wabanaki

Camp Wakpominee (Log Bay)

Camp Walden (Diamond Point)

Camp Wanakena

Chingachgook (Pilot Knob)

Corsican (Diamond Point)

Hidden Lake Girl Scout Camp

Lake George Camp

Lake George Camp for Girls

Moss Lodge

Rotary

Silver Bay Travel Camp (Silver Bay)

Skye Farm Camp

Trout Lake Camp (Bolton)

Wah-Na-Gi (Glen Eyrie)

Wa-Tah-Wah (Bolton)

Lake Hortonia

Green Mountain

Lake Kan-ac-to (Old Forge)

Adirondack Woodcraft

Lake Kushaqua

Adirondack Swim and Trip Camp

Lake Kuyrahoora

Lake Kuyrahoora Children's Camp

Lake Lauderdale

Camp Lauderdale

Lake Lucretia

Adirondack Swim Camp
Camp Boulder Point

Lake Luzerne

Camp Pine Log
Camp Tekakwitha
Luzerne Music Center
Peniel Bible Youth Camp
Song-Hawk

Lake McRorie (Long Lake)

Cedarlands

Lake Placid

Camp Askenonta (Moose Island)
Camp Birchwood
Camp Minnowbrook
Camp Solitude
Camp Treetops
Camp Undercliff
Camp Winnakee
Camp Woodsmoke
French Recreation Class for Girls
Lake Placid Camp
Lake Placid Soccer Camp

Lake Pleasant

Camp Tapawingo
Sans Souci

Lake Portaferry

Camp Portaferry

Lake St. Catherine

Camp Arrowhead
Kinikinick

Lake Vanare

Double H-Hole in the Woods Camp

Little Long Lake (Woodgate)

Nazareth

Long Lake

Adirondack Wilderness Camp
Caedmuir Lodge
Camp Beattie
Camp Onondaga
Camp Riverdale
Camp St. Mary
In-Ca-Pah-Cho
Kempchel
Long Lake Camp for the Arts
Sabattis Adventure Camp
Stonegate Music and Arts Camp
Sabattis Scout Reservation

Long Pond (Willsboro)

Camp MacCready
Camp Pok-O-Moonshine
Camp Pok-O-MacCready

Lower St. Regis Lake

Camp "Good Grief"

Lower Saranac Lake

Camp Guggenheim
Camp Rondack
Crescent Bay

Lows Lake

Sabattis Scout Reservation

Lyonsdale

Moose River Baptist Youth Camp

McCauley Pond

Camp Triangle

Massawepie Lake

Camp Massawepie
Massawepie Scout Camps

Middle Grove

Boyhaven

Moss Lake

Moss Lake Camp

North River

Northern Frontier Camp

Northville

Buck Mountain
Camp Denton
Camp Resurrection

Old Forge

The Birches
Camp Deborah
Camp Nay-A-Ti
Camp Spruce Ridge
Ga-He-Ge
Harbor Hill
Kee-Yo-No
Outlet

Osgood Lake

Lone Pine

Otter Lake

New York State Music Camp

Palmer Pond

Chepontuc

Paradox Lake

Camp Nawita
Camp Paradox
Camp Severance
Camp Woodmere
Marian Lodge
Southwoods

Parishville

Camp Vigor

Paul Smiths

Brush Hill Camp
Camp Patrick
Osgood

Piercefield

Adirondack Scout Reservation

Piseco Lake

Piseco Lake

Pottersville

Camp Cedar

Rainbow Lake (Onchiota)

Meenahga Lodge
Nokomis Lodge

Raquette Lake

Beaver Catholic Boys Camp
Camp Collier
Camp Eagle Feather
Camp Greylock
Camp Raquette (Tioga Point)
Camp Scenic
Echo Camp
Lynx Camp
Raquette Lake Boys' Camp
Raquette Lake Camps
Raquette Lake Girls' Camp
Thatcher Outpost Camp

Raquette River

Camp So-High (Long Bow)

Rollins Pond

Rollins Pond Adventure Base

Rondaxe Lake

Rondax

Round Lake

Camp Turk (Woodgate)

Sacandaga Lake

Bonheur
Camp Agaming
Camp Fowler
4-H Camp Sacandaga

Saddle Lake

Salvation Army Camp

Sagamore Lake

Sagamore Reading Camp

St. Huberts

Camp Tahawus

St. Regis Falls

St. Bernard's Summer Camp

St. Regis Lake

Maple-Wold

Saranac Lake

Camp Hendrick Hudson

Schroon Lake

Camp Cayuga
Camp Idylwold
Camp Mondamin
Camp Nahar
Camp Naomi
Camp Olowan
Camp Rainbow
Camp Red Wing
Camp Riverside
Camp Rondack
Camp Saskatchewan
Camp Sonrise
Camp Winona
Lakeside Pines
Manhattan Camp
Marble Collegiate Camp
Moon Hill
Pine Tree Camp
Schroon Lake Camp
Schroon Lodge
Schroon Nahar
Timberland

Word of Life
Wurths'

Seventh Lake

Camp Syracuse

Silver Lake

Camp Baloo
Camp Douglas
Cedar Lodge
Hawkeye Trail Camps
Silver Lake Camp

South Colton

Camp Whispering Pines

Speculator

Kun-Ja-Muk

Star Lake

Camp Hoh-Wah-Tah

Summit Lake

Camp Algonquin

Swan Lake

Ma-Ho-Ge

Thendara

Deerhurst
Nun-Da-Sah

Ticonderoga

Black Point
Carillon
Ticonderoga
Wah-Pe-Ton

Trout Pond

Camp Heathcote

Unknown

Adirondacks Summer Art School
Camp Anchorage
Camp Bradford
Log Cabin

Upper Ausable Lake

High Peaks Camp for Boys

Upper Chateaugay Lake

Adirondack Music Camp
Camp Chateaugay
Camp Chickagami
Camp Jeanne d'Arc
Camp Kairoa (or Kaiora)
Camp Lafayette
Camp Miramichi
Camp Reliance
Camp Wahalla
Chateaugay Camp Lodge
Owlyout
Tanager Lodge

Upper Saranac Lake

Camp Cherokee
Camp De Baun
Camp Navarac
Deerwood Adirondack Music Center
Forestcraft
Girl Scout Camp Eagle Island
Young Life Saranac Village

Upper St. Regis Lake

Camp Regis/Applejack
Gardner-Doing

Wakonda Lake

Camp Wakonda

Warm Pond

Kent Camp

Warren County

Ronwood

Warrensburg

Camp Echo Lake
Camp Naiweh
Crooning Pines
Forest Lake Camp
Pack Forest
Spruce Mountain
Warren County Children's Health
Camp

Westport

Meadowmount School of Music

Wheeler Pond

Camp Caravan

White Lake

Camp Russell
Grachusut
White Lake Camp

Whitehall

Twin Lakes

Whitaker Lake

Deerfoot Lodge
Kariwiyo Lodge

Willsboro

Camp Pochontas

Woodgate

Camp Oneida

Woodworth Lake

Woodworth Lake Scout Reservation

Notes

1. "Pink Music"

1. This essay draws extensively from my doctoral dissertation, which in revised form will be published as a book by New York University Press. Leslie Paris, "Children's Nature: Summer Camps in New York State, 1919–1941" (Ph.D. diss., Univ. of Michigan, 2000). I owe a debt of gratitude to the Adirondack Museum, which supported my research in the summer of 1997; to the assistance of museum staff Hallie Bond, Jim Meehan, and Jerry Pepper; and especially to the many present and former camp leaders who allowed me access to their archives and offered me a hot lunch and sometimes even accommodation for a night or two. Particular thanks are due to the helpful men and women affiliated with the following camps: Adirondack Woodcraft, Brant Lake, Che-Na-Wah, Dudley, Forest Lake, Greylock, Jeanne D'Arc, Lincoln and Whipporwill, Pok-O-Moonshine, Red Wing, Rondack, Tanager Lodge, and Treetops.

2. 1906 Camp Dudley brochure, in folder "1901–1910," Camp Dudley, Westport, New York (hereafter CD).

3. On the early history of Camp Dudley and YMCA camping, see, for instance, Minott A. Osborn, ed., *Camp Dudley: The Story of the First Fifty Years* (New York: Huntington Press, 1934); C. Howard Hopkins, *History of the YMCA in North America* (New York: Association Press, 1951), 200–207; and Eugene A. Turner, Jr., *100 Years of Y.M.C.A. Camping* (Chicago: YMCA of the USA, 1985). Until 1901, Camp Dudley served both the New York and New Jersey State YMCA committees. By 1902, all the New Jersey campers attended their own camp on Lake Wawayanda in New Jersey (where Dudley had earlier located his camp from 1886 to 1889).

4. On antimodern nostalgia and elite manhood, see, for instance, T. J. Jackson Lears, *No Place of Grace: Antimodernism and the Transformation of American Culture, 1880–1920* (New York: Pantheon, 1981); E. Anthony Rotundo, *American Manhood: Transformations in American Masculinity from the Revolution to the Modern Era* (New York: Basic Books, 1993); Gail Bederman, *Manliness and Civilization: A Cultural History of Gender and Race in the United States, 1880–1917* (Chicago: Univ. of Chicago Press, 1995); and Clifford Putney, *Muscular Christianity: Manhood and Sports in Protestant America, 1880–1920* (Cambridge, Mass.: Harvard Univ. Press, 2001).

5. On vacationing and the outdoors, see, for instance, Peter J. Schmitt, *Back to Nature: The Arcadian Myth in Urban America* (New York:

Oxford Univ. Press, 1969); John F. Sears, *Sacred Places: American Tourist Attractions in the Nineteenth Century* (New York: Oxford Univ. Press, 1989); and Cindy S. Aron, *Working at Play: A History of Vacations in the United States* (New York: Oxford Univ. Press, 1999).

6. On Adirondack industry and tourism, see Philip G. Terrie, *Contested Terrain: A New History of Nature and People in the Adirondacks* (Blue Mountain Lake and Syracuse, N.Y.: Adirondack Museum and Syracuse Univ. Press, 1997).

7. On "muscular Christianity" and turn-of-the-century boys' organizations, see, for instance, David Macleod, *Building Character in the American Boy: The Boy Scouts, Y.M.C.A. and Their Forerunners, 1870–1920* (Madison: Univ. of Wisconsin Press, 1983); Robert H. MacDonald, *Sons of the Empire: The Frontier and the Boy Scout Movement, 1890–1918* (Toronto: Univ. of Toronto Press, 1993); and Putney, *Muscular Christianity.*

8. On the early days of summer camps, see Porter Sargent, *Handbook of Summer Camps* (Boston: P. Sargent, 1924), 24–41; and H. W. Gibson's several-part series, "The History of Organized Camping," in *Camping* 8, nos. 1–7 (1936); W. Barksdale Maynard, " 'An Ideal Life in the Woods for Boys': Architecture and Culture in the Earliest Summer Camps," *Winterthur Portfolio* 34 (Spring 1999): 3–29; and Paris, "Children's Nature."

9. The earliest area camps are mentioned briefly in Sargent, *Handbook of Summer Camps,* 26. On Camp Rainbow and So-High see the camp files, Adirondack Museum, Blue Mountain Lake (hereafter AM). On Dr. Elias Brown's career and camp, see Eugene Lehman et al., eds., *Camps and Camping, For the Information and Guidance of Campers, Parents, Directors and Counsellors,* 1st ed., Spalding's Athletic Library (New York: American Sports Publishing Co., 1921), 7–8. Information about the camp's early years also appears in "Adirondack Camp for Boys" (1912), in vol. 3, uncatalogued bound volumes on camping, New York Public Library, New York City.

10. 1906 brochure, Camp So-High, AM.

11. 1914 brochure, Camp Pok-O-Moonshine, AM.

12. The cost reflected "Tuition, Books, Stationary, use of Piano, Chaperonage, Board, Laundry and Traveling expenses to Lake Placid and return to New York." See French Recreation Class for Girls, AM. On early girls' camps, see Leslie Paris, "The Adventures of Peanut and Bo: Summer

Camps and Early Twentieth Century American Girlhood," *Journal of Women's History* 12, no. 4 (Winter 2001): 47–76.

13. Sargent, *Handbook of Summer Camps,* 29, 302, 306.

14. Average wage cited in Geraldine Youcha, *Minding the Children: Child Care in America from Colonial Times to the Present* (New York: Scribner, 1995), 212. On YMCA camps of the period, see Macleod, *Building Character,* 237.

15. 1923 Camp Dudley pamphlet, folder "1923 Season," CD.

16. Information on such camps, including Camp Russell and the Warren County Children's Health Camp, appears in the AM camp files; Camp Wah-Ta-Wah is discussed in *The Lake George Mirror* 41, no. 8 (9 Aug. 1924): 15, AM.

17. "What Parents Say" (1926 brochure, Schroon Lake Camp), Schroon Lake Historical Museum, Schroon Lake, New York (hereafter SLHM).

18. Tracking the industry's growth with precision is difficult, because the majority of late-nineteenth-century and early-twentieth-century camps were not affiliated with any larger camp directors' association. One 1937 *Camping World* editorial estimated that two million American children were attending camps, out of a total of thirty million children of school age. Some children would attend camp another summer, so it is possible that as many as 15 percent of all children attended camps at some point in their childhood. Editorial, *Camping World* 3, no. 5 (May 1937): 5.

19. Rarely did area camps serve any but white campers. Camp Pok-O-Moonshine was atypical, in that founder Charles Robinson originally planned his camp with the needs of some of his Central American boarding school patrons (for whom the trip back home was too long) in mind. In the 1930s, a few of the Camp Riverdale boys were Asian American. The staff, on the other hand, was often more diverse, in that many white-only camps had African American cooks.

20. This typical phrasing appears in the 1924 Lake George Camp brochure, 6, vertical files, AM. Several camps associated with urban schools represented an exception to the practice of religious segregation; Camp Riverdale and the North Country Camps, for instance, both drew religiously mixed clienteles from New York City feeder schools.

21. Rabbi Isaac Moses (1847–1926) was one of the charter members of the Central Conference of American Rabbis, and was well known in Reform circles. The conference's *Union Prayer Book* of 1894 was based upon his self-published 1892 manuscript. See the memoriam in *The Reform Advocate* 73, no. 23 (9 July 1927), SLHM.

22. Most Schroon-area camps served a fairly acculturated clientele. Others, like Camp Swastika near Old Forge and Camp Che-Na-Wah near Minerva, promised kosher food. Sargent, *Handbook of Summer Camps,* 310; *Che-Na-Wit* 3, no. 1 (16 July 1927), in untitled scrapbook (1920s), collection of Camp Che-Na-Wah, Minerva, New York. On Schroon Lake-area camps and their clients, see Leslie Paris, "A Home Though Away from Home": Brooklyn Jews and Interwar Children's Summer Camps," in Ilana Abramovitch and Séan Galvin, eds., *Jews of Brooklyn* (Hanover, N.H.: Univ. Press of New England, 2001), 242–49.

23. Sargent, *Handbook of Summer Camps,* 301.

24. William Steckel, quoted in Elizabeth Chisholm Abbott, ed., *Remembering Woodcraft, by Campers and Councilors over 50 Years* (Old Forge, N.Y.: Adirondack Woodcraft Camps, 1975), 49; Adirondack Woodcraft Camps, AM.

25. For example, at the turn of the twentieth century, the thirty New York City boys who headed off to Camp So-High spent almost a full twenty-four hours traveling to camp; they first traveled upstate by train to Potsdam, then were driven twenty miles, and finally they boarded canoes for the last mile's journey. *Camp So-High in the Adirondacks* (1906), and letter from Carl Coit, 31 Mar. 1906, in Camp So-High file, AM.

26. Photographs dated 1928 and 1932, folder 3, Camp Severance photograph collection, AM.

27. "The Bee-Ell-See" (1925), collection of Brant Lake Camp, Brant Lake, New York.

28. "Rondacts 1936," SLHM.

29. Camp Riverdale *Stag and Eagle* 4, no. 3, 28 Aug. 1940, file 19, box 2, Camp Riverdale MS 70–12, AM.

30. "Annual Spring Number," *Dudley Doings* (1922), CD.

31. "Che-Na-Wit 1929," 2 Aug. 1929, in scrapbook, untitled (1920s), collection of Camp Che-Na-Wah, Minerva, New York.

32. Seton's ideas were popularized in his self-published *The Red Book; Or, How to Play Indian* (1904). Later scholarly attention to Indian mimicry appears in Jay Mechling, " 'Playing Indian' and the Search for Authenticity in Modern White America," *Prospects* 5 (1980): 17–33; and Rayna Green, "The Tribe Called Wannabee: Playing Indian in America and Europe," *Folklore* 99, no. 1 (1988): 30–55. The fullest discussion of Indian play and summer camp ideals is articulated in Philip J. Deloria, *Playing Indian: Otherness and Authenticity in the Assumption of American Indian Identity* (New Haven: Yale Univ. Press, 1998).

33. Robert Pfaff, cited in Abbott, *Remembering Woodcraft,* 30. "Woodcraft" camps in the region included Camp Mohican (Hague, 1909), Camp Tahawus (St. Huberts, 1924), Tanager Lodge (Merrill, 1925), and Camp Snowy Mountain (Sabael, 1930).

34. 1928 brochure, Camp Ticonderoga, AM.

35. 1933 brochure, "Camp Pok-O-Moonshine in the Adirondacks," collection of Camp Pok-O-Moonshine, Willsboro, New York (hereafter POM). Camp Dudley moved to its present location in 1908; thus Camp Pok-O-Moonshine, founded in 1906, is the oldest extant Adirondack Camp on its original site.

36. Herbert McAneny, "Cold River Idylls, 1916–1962," Adirondack Mountain Club, Aug. 1989, 10, AM.

37. Camper comments, file 29, box 2, Camp Riverdale, MS 70–12, AM.

38. "The Chronicle," 1936–1937 (1936 season), 31, SLHM.

39. "Historical and Indian Pageant" (1915), "1901–1910," and *Dudley Doings,* 21 July 1921, CD.

40. "Camp Lincoln for Boys, Camp Whippoorwill for Girls, in the Adirondacks, 1937," collection of North Country Camps, Keeseville, New York.

41. Brad Konkler, interview by author, 2 Oct. 1997; Franz Geierhaas, "Interview with Helen Haskell," collection of Camp Treetops, Lake Placid, New York. The directors of the coeducational Camp Treetops studied with Dewey at Columbia University.

42. "Camp Dudley Leader's Manual," "1932 Season," CD.

43. 1906 brochure, "Camp So-High in the Adirondacks," and letter from Carl Coit, 31 Mar. 1906, in Camp So-High file, AM.

44. J. R. to Willie, 14 Feb. 1977, "Memories: Tents to Cabins," CD.

45. P. to Willie, 13 Feb. 1977, and M. to Willie, undated, "Memories," CD.

46. *Dudley Doings,* 2 July 1930, CD.

47. M. to Willie, "Memories," CD.

48. Welch to Marcia Smith, 22 Feb. 1968, Tanager Lodge, AM.

49. Edward M. Cameron, quoted in "Those Elysian Fields: Camp Pok-O-Moonshine's First Fifty Years," 10, POM.

"Pink Music" Sidebars

S1. LuAnne Gaykowski Kozma, former camper at Girl Scout Camp Eagle Island, to the Adirondack Museum Camp Memories project, 2004.

2. "A Paradise for Boys and Girls"

1. One such quotation appears in Abigail Van Slyck, "Housing the Happy Camper," *Minnesota History,* Summer 2002, 68; she found the quote in Herbert Twining, "Camps of Fifty Years Ago," *Nation's Schools* 21 (Apr. 1938): 18, who dates the original remark to 1922 and the author as Harvard president Charles Eliot.

2. For a discussion of the Murray phenomenon, see Warder Cadbury, introduction to *Adventures in the Wilderness,* by William H. H. Murray, ed. William K. Verner (Blue Mountain Lake and Syracuse, N.Y.: Adirondack Museum and Syracuse Univ. Press, 1970).

3. Charles Loring Brace (?), editorial in *New York Times,* 9 Aug. 1864.

4. Cadbury, introduction to *Adventures,* by Murray, 42–44.

5. Eugene A. Turner, Jr., *YMCA Camping: An Abbreviated History* (Chicago: Young Men's Christian Association of the United States, 1984), 15; Thomas Hale et al., eds., *Camp Dudley: The First Hundred Years* (Westport, NY: Camp Dudley, 1984), 5–9. In 1892 Sumner Dudley was named the first secretary for "boy's work."

6. See W. Barksdale Maynard, " 'An Ideal Life in the Woods for Boys': Architecture and Culture in the Earliest Summer Camps," *Winterthur Portfolio* 34, no. 1 (Spring 1999): 3–7, for a complete discussion of the layout and influence of Camp Chocorua. Balch was ultimately not successful in creating a lasting institution; the camp closed in 1889.

7. "Brant Lake Camp," ca. 1965, n.p., Adirondack Museum Library (hereafter AML).

8. John M. Johansen, *A Vacation on Purpose: Camp of the Woods, 1900–1980* (Speculator, N.Y.: Gospel Volunteers, 1980), 70–71. The YMCA had been founded in London in 1844 with the aim of helping young men adapt to life in the big city. In particular, it was concerned with the spiritual development of the large numbers of young men who were moving to the city from rural areas where they had had more oversight and more support. By the 1890s the movement was firmly entrenched in the United States. The men's division of Camp Iroquois disappeared in 1914 when the camp outgrew its site and moved to Speculator, where it is still in business as Camp-of-the-Woods.

9. "The Catholic Summer School of America," 1914, 39, private collection.

10. Allen Hackett, *Quickened Spirit: A Biography of Frank Sutliff Hackett* (New York: The Riverdale Country School, 1957), 91.

11. C. T. Ludington, *Memoirs of The Ransom (Adirondack-Florida) School.* Privately printed, 1968. Collection of Ransom Everglades School, Coconut Grove, Florida.

12. Until the middle of the twentieth century, when successful drug treatment for "consumption" was developed, both prevention and treatment commonly included sleeping with the windows open.

13. Van Slyck, "Housing," 73.

14. "Camp Dudley," *Association Boys,* June 1905, 9.

15. "Camp Pok-O-Moonshine in the Adirondacks" (1914), 7, AML. Abigail Van Slyck, "Kitchen Technologies and Mealtime Rituals: Interpreting the Food Axis at American Summer Camps, 1890–1950," *Technology and Culture* 43, no. 4 (Oct. 2002), discusses "rebuilding the health of urban children" as one of the explicit benefits of camp, particularly during the nutrition scares of the second decade of the twentieth century.

16. "The Catholic Summer School of America," 39.

17. H. Tilden Swan, "Recollections of Camp Pok-O-Moonshine," privately printed for Camp Pok-O-Moonshine, 1978, 5, AML.

18. Swan, "Recollections," 5.

19. MacLeod, *Building Character,* 81. Gulick was an important figure in the early years of camping, as we shall see.

20. Camp Pok-O-Moonshine photograph album, private collection.

21. The picture was taken at a camp leadership course field study week, at either the Girl Scout Camp Andrée Clark or at the Bear Mountain Inn.

22. Paris, "Children's Nature," 51–52, discusses Progressive-era reformers and their concerns about children; see 148–49 for Dewey's contribution.

23. Ruth Timm, *Raquette Lake: A Time to Remember* (Utica, N.Y.: North Country Books, 1989), 181.

24. See Macleod, *Building Character,* 121, for a discussion of Progressivism, the Boy Scouts, and the YMCA.

25. The Camp Directors' Association also absorbed the National Association of Directors of Girls Camps (1916) and the Midwestern Camp Directors Association (1921) to form the American Camping Association. See Arthur T. Wilcox, "Organized Camping in New York State" (Master's thesis, New York State College of Forestry, Syracuse Univ., 1941).

26. "Camp Leadership Course," *Teachers College Bulletin,* 11th ser., no. 12 (14 Feb. 1920). See also Wilcox, "Organized Camping," 20.

27. A fascinating and prickly character, Seton has been discussed and assessed in a number of different contexts, none of which really explores his influence on organized camping. See Betty Keller, *Black Wolf: The Life of Ernest Thompson Seton* (Vancouver, B.C.: Douglas and MacIntyre, 1984); and John Henry Wadland, *Ernest Thompson Seton: Man in Nature and the Progressive Era, 1880–1915* (New York: Arno Press, 1978). H. Allen Anderson calls him a "Progressive social reformer" in his article "Ernest Thompson Seton and the Woodcraft Indians," *Journal of American Culture* 8, no. 1 (1987): 43.

28. Untitled autobiographical essay by Julian Harris Salomon, 1928, private collection.

29. Ernest Thompson Seton, *The Book of Woodcraft* (Garden City, N.J.: Garden City Publishing Co, 1912), 4–6.

30. Anderson, "Seton," 44.

31. Within a few months of beginning his medical career at the Pine Ridge Agency in South Dakota, Eastman was called on to treat the survivors of the massacre at Wounded Knee. See Penelope Kelsey, "A 'Real Indian' to the Boy Scouts: Charles Eastman as a Resistance Writer," *Western American Literature* 38, no. 1 (2003): 30–48. See also Deloria, *Playing Indian,* 122–24.

32. Wadland, *Seton,* 326.

33. Anderson, "Ernest Thompson Seton," 46.

34. Wadland, 151, claims that girls were not admitted until after Woodcraft was reorganized in 1915, but Salomon dates girls' membership at least as early as 1905. Julian Harris Salomon, "Three Great Scouts and a Lady," unpublished ms., private collection, 48.

35. Salomon, "Three Great Scouts," 47.

36. Clara Barrus, *Life and Letters of John Burroughs,* 1925, quoted in Salomon, "Three Scouts," with no further information. Burroughs's kind words may have been in part an effort to smooth over the harsh criticism he had leveled at Seton for what Burroughs felt was too much sentimentalism and claims of animal intelligence in Seton's nature writings. The "nature faker" controversy, in which Roosevelt played a large part, is covered in Ralph H. Lutts, *The Nature Fakers: Wildlife, Science and Sentiment* (Golden, Colo.: Fulcrum Publishing, 1990).

37. Keller, *Black Wolf,* 165–72.

38. The tale of Seton's ouster from the Boy Scouts of America has been told in several places; see Keller, *Black Wolf,* 174–78.

39. Ibid., 49.

40. Macleod and Wadland dismiss the Woodcraft movement as having had little acceptance beyond the Camp Fire Girls and the YMCA, and most historians treat the movement only as a precursor or ultimately unsuccessful alternative to the Boy Scouts. Wadland, *Seton,* 302.

41. "Woodcraft League of America, Inc., Scroll of Authority," 1927, private collection.

42. Paris, "Children's Nature," 29–31, contains a discussion of Hall and his influence, arguing that Dewey himself was not a proponent of this aspect of Hall's work.

43. Ibid.

44. Macleod, *Building Character,* 242.

45. Barbara Vosburgh, letter to author, 23 Sept. 2003.

46. Susan Scher, letter to author, 21 Mar. 2004. See also Paris, "Children's Nature," 54–55, for more on the Fresh Air Fund and the Harriman Park camps.

47. The first Jewish camp in the country was the Surprise Lake Camp in Maine, founded by the Young Men's Hebrew Association in 1902. This discussion of the Schroon Lake Camp and early Jewish camping is largely taken from Paris, "Children's Nature," 105–6.

48. Libby Raynes Adelman, interview with author, Camp Greylock, 11 July 2001.

49. Leslie Paris traces the beginnings of the girls' camp movement, starting with two New York State boys' camps that began admitting girls in the early 1890s. The Luther Gulick Camps in Maine and Kehonka in New Hampshire, both founded in 1902 after the Lake Placid venture, are generally given the credit for being the first exclusively girls' camps in the country. Paris, "Children's Nature," 38–39.

50. "French Vacation Class for Girls at Lake Placid, Adirondacks," 1896, AML.

51. Paris, "Children's Nature," 39, quotes much the same material from the Adirondack Museum brochure.

52. *The Delightful and Healthful Resorts Reached by the Delaware and Hudson Railroad* (Albany: D&H Co., 1909), n.p.

53. Nina Hart, "And Thirty: An Adventure in Camping," typescript, n.d., n.p., AML

54. Ibid.

55. See Deloria, *Playing Indian,* 111–13; and Paris, "Children's Nature," 46–47, for the story of the founding of the Camp Fire Girls.

56. As the YMCA's first International Secretary for Physical Work, Gulick promoted physical training for boys and gymnasiums for local Y's. In 1895 he proposed the now-famous red triangle for the YMCA, symbolizing the physical, mental, and spiritual aspects of the whole man that the YMCA aimed to develop. MacLeod, *Building Character,* 72.

57. Mary Ellen Putnam, "The History of Children's Camps on Chateaugay Lake," brochure printed for the Fifth Annual Chateaugay Lakes Arts Association, 2003, 10. Camping history usually names Laura Garrett, a Progressive educator, as the founder of the first coeducational camp in the country.

58. Wilcox, "Organized Camping," 18.

59. Creighton Peet, "What Is 'Wilderness Camping'?" *American Forests,* Nov. 1955, offprint, n.p. Peet's example of a wilderness camp was Tanager Lodge.

60. Lutts, *Nature Fakers,* 26–31, is a good summary of the movement, which had its basis in the popularity of outdoor recreation, growing concerns about conservation of resources, and natural theology (seeing the greatness of God in the works of nature).

61. Seton, *Book of Woodcraft,* 3–4.

62. Excerpt from the 29 July 1939 *Gwunduk* in *Noosanwit and Gwunduk,* Summer 1995, 7; *Noosanwit and Gwunduk,* Summer 1997, 3.

63. "Adirondack Woodcraft Camps," 1928 brochure, n.p., AML.

64. Peet, "Wilderness Camping."

65. Ann Wallace McKendry, letter to author, 30 May 2004.

66. Charles L. Brayton, "The 1914 'Fast Marcy,'" *Adirondac,* May-June 1968.

67. Peter Gucker, letter to author, 24 Feb. 2004.

68. American Red Cross, "The Development of First Aid, Life Saving, Water Safety and Accident Prevention," 1950. The author thanks Brien Williams, historian, American Red Cross, for this reference.

69. Adelman interview, 11 July 2001.

70. John Leach, letter to author, 24 Feb. 2004.

71. "The Adirondack Camp for Boys," 1906, AML.

72. "Camp Pok-O-Moonshine," 11.

73. Swan, "Recollections," 5.

74. George H. Longstaff, *From Heyday to Mayday* (St. Petersburg, Fla.: Valkyrie Publishing House, 1983), 77.

75. *Old Town Canoes,* 1910 catalog, 29, AML.

76. Adirondack Museum accession files, 2002.2.

77. Waterfront director's notebook, Camp Navarac mss., AML.

78. Adelman interview, 11 July 2001.

79. Camps Navarac, Jeanne d'Arc, Echo, Tapawingo, and Girl Scout Camp Eagle Island all had versions of this ceremony.

80. Billy Collins, "The Lanyard," *Five Points* 7, no. 1 (Fall 2003): 7.

81. Putnam "Children's Camps on Chateaugay," 3, quotes an article in the 1905 *Chateaugay Record and Franklin County Democrat* about Walhalla.

82. *The Paradoxian,* 1913, 2–3, AML.

83. Robert Gersten, *The Spirit of Ole Brant Lake* (Chapel Hill, N.C.: Chapel Hill Press, 2000), 11. Richard Rodgers was a camper at the Schroon Lake Camp.

84. Hale, *Camp Dudley,* 28. Camp cooks well into the twentieth century were often black because few other good jobs were available to African Americans. Paris, *Children's Nature,* 255–58, discusses camp minstrel shows at length.

85. Seton, *Book of Woodcraft,* 191.

86. David Nemzer, letter to author, 27 Aug. 2002.

87. Adirondack Museum accession file 96.43. Nawita (Paradox Lake), where Navarac founder Sara Blum worked before Navarac, as well as Woodmere (Paradox), awarded letters for pillows as well.

88. Macleod, *Building Character,* 125.

89. Minott A. Osborn, ed., *Camp Dudley,* 185–86.

90. John Leach, letter to author, 25 Feb. 2004.

91. Jerry Cowle, "As I Did It," *Sports Illustrated,* 23 May 1977. The swastika is an ancient symbol in several cultures; the Scouts used it because of its association with American Indians.

92. Peter Gucker, letter to author, 9 Mar. 2004. Lincoln's Indian pageants had been discontinued by World War II.

93. Excerpt from *Gwunduk,* 17 July 1937, reprinted in *Noosanwit and Gwunduk,* the newsletter of the Red Wing/Red Cloud Alumnae Association, Summer 1997, 3, AML.

94. Paris, "Children's Nature," 274; Alan Jones, letter to author, 30 Apr. 2004; Oren Lyons, telephone interview with author, 23 June 2004. See also Deloria, *Playing Indian.*

95. Gersten, *Ole Brant Lake,* 19. Gersten admits that Brant Lake "stole" some elements of Color War from Camp Paradox, where the founders had been counselors.

96. "Boating Meet War Week 1969," waterfront director's notebook, Camp Navarac mss., AML.

97. See Paris, "Children's Nature," 105–22, for a complete discussion of Jewish camping in New York State; and Jenna Weissmann Joselit, "The Jewish Way of Play," in *A Worthy Use of Summer: Jewish Summer Camping in America* (Philadelphia: The National Museum of Jewish History, 1993), 15–28. Camp Swastika was certainly named for the Plains Indian symbol and was out of business before the symbol acquired a much more sinister association.

98. See Paris, "Children's Nature," 138–51, section entitled "Creating Community Through Space and Time."

99. *The Paradoxian* 4 no. 2 (Aug. 1913): 7, AML.

100. Dean Pohl interview with author, Raquette Lake, 15 Nov. 2003.

101. Paris, "Children's Nature," finds the conflict between modernity and rusticity and nostalgia a major theme in the development of camping between the world wars.

102. Van Slyck, "Housing," 69–83. See also Paris, "Children's Nature," 211–16.

103. Van Slyck, 74, dates the Camp Director's Association's endorsement of cabins as the mid-1920s.

104. Wilcox, "Organized Camping," 89.

105. "French Vacation Class," n. p.

106. Silver Lake Camp mss., AML.

107. Tim Shea, New York State Board of Health, letter to author, 5 Aug. 2003.

108. "Kellogg's Manual for Summer Camps," 1937, n.p., AML.

109. Carlton Clough, letter to author, 24 June 2003.

110. Gail Bosch, interview with author, Blue Mountain Lake, New York, 23 July 2002.

111. "Camp Che-Na-Wah," 1923, 7, private collection.

112. Riverdale ms., "Trips" folder, 15–20 Aug. 1938, AML.

113. Silver Lake mss., trip menus file, AML.

114. Phillip H. Smith, Sr., to Jerold Pepper, 2 Jan. 2003, AML.

115. My thanks to Joan Jacobs Brumberg for suggesting Little League as an example; figures are from the 2004 Little League website (<www.littleleague.org/history>).

116. This is excluding the Scout camps established during the period.

117. In the 1930s and 1940s, after the movement lost credibility as a national force after the Scopes "Monkey Trial," it turned inwards, in a sense, and instead of fighting national, high-profile fights against bolshevism and evolutionary theory, it "was transformed from a national movement into a subculture, Bible institutes, radio stations, summer camps, and related institutions gradually emerged as the new bastions of faith."

Niels Bjerre-Poulson, "The Transformation of the Fundamentalist Movement, 1925–1942," *American Studies in Scandinavia* 20 (1988): 97.

118. *Celebration: Fifty Faithful Years* (Schroon Lake, N.Y.: Word of Life Fellowship, 1989); and Wayne Lewis, letter to author, 1 Mar. 2004.

119. Paul Pillis, letter to author, 16 Oct. 2002.

120. Robert F. Swift, *Music from the Mountains: New York State Music Camp, 1947–1996* (Plymouth, N.H., 1996), 17.

121. "Moss Lake Camp," 1945, n.p., AML.

122. Ibid.

123. "Camp Minnowbrook," ca. 1963, catalog, AML.

124. Leonard Gerber, letter to author, 28 Jan. 2003.

125. George and Jane Linck, interview with author, 21 Jan. 2003.

126. A 46er is someone who had climbed all the forty-six peaks in the Adirondacks that are more than four thousand feet in elevation.

127. Mark Dollard, interview with author, 10 Oct. 2002; see also Robert Paul, "Historical Notes: Association of Adirondack Scout Camps," 1992, private collection.

128. I am greatly indebted to Jenna Weissman Joselit for her help in an interview, 26 Mar. 2004. See also Joselit, 15–28; and Daniel Issacman, "Jewish Summer Camps in the United States and Canada, 1900–1969," Ph.D. diss., Dropsie Univ., 1970.

129. Hale, *Camp Dudley,* 134.

130. Ibid., 129–35.

131. Karen Meltzer, interview with author, 5 Apr. 2004.

132. Arlene Hirschfelder et al., *American Indian Stereotypes in the World of Children: A Reader and Bibliography,* 2nd ed. (Lanham, Md.: Scarecrow Press, 1999), 83.

133. Correspondence with Peter Gucker, North Country Camps, 9 Mar. 2004.

134. New York State Department of Environmental Conservation, "A Short History of the DEC Environmental Camp Program," n.d., AML.

135. Wadland, 353.

136. New York State Camp Directors Association, "The Economic Impact of Summer Camps in New York State," 1996, AML.

137. I am indebted to Karen Meltzer of the Brant Lake Camp for this insight.

138. See sidebar at the beginning of this essay.

"A Paradise for Boys and Girls" Sidebars

S1. "Camp Riverdale in the Adirondacks" (1932), AMVF.

S2. Quoted without reference in *Camp Riverdale, 35th Anniversary,* 1947, n.p., private collection. Leslie Paris noted the same quotation in an earlier Riverdale brochure (1932) in the Adirondack Museum's collection; Paris, "Children's Nature," 203.

S3. "Adirondack Camp for Boys," 1906 brochure, n.p., AML. Quoted in Paris, "Children's Nature," 38. Ernest Balch also identified the summer resort as typical of the "problem of summer" for parents of boys.

S4. "The Adirondack Camp," 1906 catalog, n.p., AMVF.

S5. Camper Archibald Ormond, quoted in "Those Elysian Fields: Camp Pok-O-Moonshine's First Fifty Years," 1955, 7.

S6. "The Camp Song," written by Eddie Cameron, 1916, in *Those Elysian Fields: Pok-O-MacCready, 1905–2004,* ed. Anne Smith, 18.

S7. "Camp Riverdale" (ca. 1937), n.p., private collection.

S8. Porter Sargent, *A Handbook for Private School Teachers* (Boston: Porter Sargent, 1930), 276. Deming was a member of the Child Study Association, incorporated in 1924.

S9. Eugene F. Moses, "Camping Is Living," in *The Chronicle,* Schroon Lake Camp, 1940, 3. Moses was the son of Schroon Lake Camp founder Isaac Moses and followed his father as director.

S10. Ernest Thompson Seton, "The Woodcraft Idea," in *The Birch-Bark Roll of Woodcraft,* 24th ed., 1927, www.inquiry.net/traditional/seton/birch.

S11. Seton, *Book of Woodcraft,* 4–6.

S12. Quoted in Salomon, "Three Scouts," 49.

S13. Peet, "Wilderness Camping."

S14. Eugene F. Moses, foreword in *The Camp Chronicle* (Schroon Lake Camp, 1935), 3.

S15. "French Vacation Class for Girls at Lake Placid, Adirondacks" 1896, AML.

S16. Hale, *Camp Dudley,* 66–69. For Schroon Lake boys' patriotism, see Paris, "Children's Nature," 147.

S17. *The Camp Chronicle* (Schroon Lake Camp) 11, no. 3 (1918): 11.

S18. "Adirondack Woodcraft Camps," 1928 brochure, n.p., AML.

S19. "Report of the Nature Club," Camp Dudley, 1922, Camp Dudley Archives.

S20. "Adirondack Woodcraft Camps."

S21. "Camp Dudley," *Association Boys,* June 1905, 10.

S22. "Raquette Lake Boys' Club," 1917 brochure, 2, private collection.

S23. Waterfront director's notebook, Navarac mss., AML.

S24. "Camp Che-Na-Wah," 1923 brochure, 9, private collection.

S25. Naomi Levine, letter to parents, Camp Greylock, Sept. 1959, private collection.

S26. "Camp Riverdale," 1960, n. p., private collection.

S27. Poem by James Spencer Taylor, Camp Riverdale Collection, AML 70–12, folder 41.

S28. "Meenahga Lodge" brochure (1930–32), n. p., collection of the Ransom-Everglades School.

S29. Plaque in Adirondack Museum collection, 2000.34.19. Moss Lake's Honor Girl Creed was written by camper Evelyn MacDonald in 1929.

S30. Lincoln Barnett to Leon Barnett, Camp Dudley, 26 June 1923, private collection.

S31. Camp Greylock songbook, ca. 1965, private collection.

S32. Camp Woodmere songbook, 1980, AML.

S33. Mark Burstein to the Adirondack Museum Camp Memories Project, 2004.

S34. Wilcox, "Organized Camping," 88, 141.

S35. "Camp Che-Na-Wah," 1923, 3.

S36. Lincoln Barnett to Leon Barnett, July 1924, private collection.

S37. "Camp Che-Na-Wah" 1923, 7.

S38. Adam Brumberg to Mr. and Mrs. David Brumberg, 1974, private collection.

S39. "Lori" to her parents from Camp Greylock, private collection.

S40. John F. Buyce, mayor of Speculator, to George F. Tibbetts [*sic*], 10 Aug. 1935, AMVF

S41. Longstaff, *Heyday,* 77–94.

S42. Barbara Schuman Eckmann, interview with author, 3 Apr. 2003.

S43. Paris, "Children's Nature," 75–77.

S44. Camp foundation dates are more common than dates camps closed. Figures given are for definite known dates. See introductory note on sources in the appendix.

S45. Buyce to Tibbitts, 1935; and Pohl interview, 2003.

S46. Eckmann interview.

S47. Maitland deSormo, in *Summers on the Saranacs* (Saranac Lake, N.Y.: Adirondack Yesteryears, 1980), 283, quotes Camp La Jeunesse director Hank Blagden in a 1940 letter to the editor of the La Jeunesse newsletter.

S48. "Excerpts from Keynote Address," Annual Convention of the Association of Private Camps, 4–7, Feb. 1959, AML.

S49. Sung to the tune of "Happy Talk" from *South Pacific,* the 1949 Rodgers and Hammerstein musical, from the counselor show, Camp Greylock, Greylock scrapbooks, private collection.

S50. "Deerwood Adirondack Music Center," 1952 brochure, n.p., Saranac Lake Free Library.

S51. Susan "Brownie" Brown to the Adirondack Museum Camp Memories Project, 2004.

S52. My thanks to John Leach of the Adirondack Woodcraft Camps for his insights on this.

S53. Naomi Levine, letter to parents, 3 Oct. 1960, private collection.

S54. Copyright Allan Sherman, 1963.

S55. Megan Hughes to the Adirondack Museum Camp Memories project, 2004.

3. "A Wiser and Safer Place"

"A Wiser and Safer Place" Sidebars

S1. "Camping Forward" was written by Frederick Lewis, director of the Vistamont Camps in Bristol, New Hampshire. Marjorie Cooper, Cleveland Campfire Girls executive, set it to music for *Camping Magazine.* I am grateful to Joan Jacobs Brumberg for finding the song in *Camping* for January 1943.

S2. Bart Hewitt, former Undercliff camper, to the Adirondack Museum Camp Memories project, 2004.

Sources and Further Reading

THE HISTORY of organized children's camping has only recently come to the attention of scholars studying childhood and education. Camping enthusiasts (mostly former "happy campers") have written histories of individual camps and books of reminiscences. The original documents of organized camping—the catalogs, counselor's notebooks, letters home, and photographs—tend to be inaccessible to all but the scholar with lots of time on his or her hands and access to the attics of camp buildings and local historical societies. Between the dissertations and the "memory books," however, the general reader will find little on the subject. It is in the hope of filling that gap that the Adirondack Museum and Syracuse University Press have published this book.

Readers wishing to know more about the context in which children's camping evolved should read the most recent comprehensive work on the history of the Adirondack Park, Philip G. Terrie's *Contested Terrain: A New History of Nature and People in the Adirondacks* (Blue Mountain Lake and Syracuse, N.Y.: Adirondack Museum and Syracuse Univ. Press, 1997). In addition, several older works on the subject are still helpful, among them Frank Graham's *The Adirondack Park: A Political History* (New York: Knopf, 1978); and William H. H. Murray's *Adventures in the Wilderness,* ed. William K. Verner (Blue Mountain Lake and Syracuse, N.Y.: Adirondack Museum and Syracuse Univ. Press) 1970. For background on the use of Indian culture, Philip J. Deloria, *Playing Indian: Otherness and Authenticity in the Assumption of American Indian Identity* (New Haven: Yale Univ. Press, 1998) is invaluable. For the story of the nature study movement, see Ralph H. Lutts's *The Nature Fakers: Wildlife, Science and Sentiment* (Golden, Colo.: Fulcrum Publishing, 1990).

The long essay in this book, "A Paradise for Boys and Girls," draws heavily from Leslie Paris's doctoral dissertation, "Children's Nature: Summer Camps in New York State, 1919–1941" (Univ. of Michigan, 2000). Dr. Paris was academic consultant for the exhibit that preceded this book; it opened in 2003 and had the same name. Paris also wrote a research report that informed that exhibit. Susan A. Miller's "Girls in Nature/The Nature of Girls: Transforming Female Adolescence at Summer Camp,

1900–1939" (Ph.D. diss., Univ. of Pennsylvania, 2001) focuses on girls' camps in a wider geographical area. Daniel Issacman's "Jewish Summer Camps in the United States and Canada, 1900–1969" (Ph.D. diss., Dropsie Univ., 1970) can be read today as a primary source, given that Issacman was interested in surveying the effectiveness of Jewish camps in educating children in Jewish culture. Even older but of use for learning about New York camping is Arthur T. Wilcox's "Organized Camping in New York State" (MS thesis, New York State College of Forestry, Syracuse Univ., 1941).

The few broader histories available to a general audience include Eleanor Eells's *A History of Organized Camping* (Martinsville, IN: The American Camping Association, 1986). Eells, a camping professional, was personally acquainted with many of the people involved in the movement during the 1920s and later. The YMCA has published a small book about its pioneering work in children's camping: Eugene A. Turner Jr., *YMCA Camping: An Abbreviated History* (Chicago: Young Men's Christian Assoc. of the United States, 1984). The National Museum of American Jewish History did an exhibit on Jewish summer camping and a companion catalog containing critical scholarship: Jenna Weissman Joselit and Karen S. Mittleman, eds., *A Worthy Use of Summer: Jewish Summer Camping in America* (Philadelphia: National Museum of American Jewish History, 1993).

Scholars are beginning to study various aspects of children's camping. W. Barksdale Maynard's " 'An Ideal Life in the Woods for Boys,' Architecture and Culture in the Earliest Summer Camps," *Winterthur Portfolio* 34, no. 1 (Spring 1999), looks at the built environment, as does Abigail Van Slyck's "Housing the Happy Camper," *Minnesota History,* Summer 2002, 68–83. Van Slyck has also studied camp foodways: "Kitchen Technologies and Mealtime Rituals: Interpreting the Food Axis at American Summer Camps, 1890–1950," *Technology and Culture* 43, no. 4 (Oct. 2002).

Organized camping for children grew out of a wider movement to improve the education and character of America's youth, a subject that has received attention from historians. David MacLeod gives a comprehensive background in his book *Building Character in the American Boy: The Boy Scouts, YMCA, and Their*

Forerunners, 1870–1920 (Madison: Univ. of Wisconsin Press, 1983), although it has little to say about girls.

Ernest Thompson Seton was an influential figure in the early twentieth-century youth movement whose impact on organized camping has not been fully explored. Readers interested in Seton could start with his *Birch-Bark Roll of the Woodcraft Indians* (New York: Brieger Press, 1902), now very rare, or *The Book of Woodcraft* (Garden City, N.J.: Garden City Publishing Co., 1912 and subsequent years). Betty Keller's *Black Wolf: The Life of Ernest Thompson Seton* (Vancouver, B.C.: Douglas and MacIntyre, 1984) is a biography, and John Henry Wadland's *Ernest Thompson Seton: Man in Nature and the Progressive Era, 1880–1915* (New York: Arno Press, 1978) places Seton in context. H. Allen Anderson's article "Ernest Thompson Seton and the Woodcraft Indians," *Journal of American Culture* 8, no. 1 (1987): 43–50, is a shorter piece that is also helpful.

Many individual camps have written their own histories, although not many are generally available. Among those used in this book are: Minott A. Osborn, ed., *Camp Dudley: The Story of the First Fifty Years* (New York: Huntington Press, 1934); Thomas Hale et al., eds., *Camp Dudley: The First Hundred Years* (Westport, N.Y.: Camp Dudley, 1984); John M. Johansen, *A Vacation on Purpose: Camp of the Woods, 1900–1980* (Speculator, N.Y.: Gospel Volunteers, 1980); Allen Hackett, *Quickened Spirit: A Biography of Frank Sutliff Hackett* (New York: The Riverdale Country School, 1957); George H. Longstaff, *From Heyday to Mayday* (St. Petersburg, Fla.: Valkyrie Publishing House, 1983); Robert Gersten, *The Spirit of Ole Brant Lake* (Chapel Hill, N.C.: Chapel Hill Press, 2000); *Celebration: Fifty Faithful Years* (Schroon Lake: Word of

Life Fellowship, 1989); and Robert F. Swift, *Music from the Mountains: New York State Music Camp, 1947–1996* (Plymouth, N.H.: NYSMC Press, 1996).

Publications of evocative reminiscences include Laurie Susan Kahn's *Sleepaway: The Girls of Summer and the Camps They Love* (New York: Workman Publishing, 2003); and Richard J. S. Gutman and Kellie O. Gutman's *The Summer Camp Memory Book* (New York: Crown Publishing Co., 1983). Photographer Barbara Morgan's *Summer's Children: A Photographic Cycle of Life at Camp* (Scarsdale, N.Y.: Morgan and Morgan, 1951) portrays Camp Treetops and contains an introduction by Helen Haskell, then director of Treetops, discussing the place of camping in American education in the 1950s.

Readers may wonder about our authority for specific camp statistics and tidbits of information, particularly while reading the appendix. It would be far too tedious, both to the authors and to the readers, to cite every guidebook, map reference, letter, and catalog from which much of this information was gleaned. If such a reference is missing, however, the reader can assume it can be found in the Children's Camp Files at the Adirondack Museum. These files were created in the course of this project, and will be deposited in the Adirondack Museum Library at its conclusion.

At the time of this printing, the Children's Camps Memory Project, a website that contains the material in the appendix and on which people may leave memories and comments about specific camps, is still up and running. It is, by its nature, ephemeral, however, and when it is taken down the material it recorded will be printed and filed in the library files.

Index